高校英语选修课系列教材

MASTERING ENGLISH
PUBLIC SPEAKING
A PROGRESSIVE APPROACH

英语公众演讲进阶教程

总主编　赵　玲
主　编　谢晓梅　刘　莹　鲁亚侠
副主编　陆　朋　卢醒春　吴小红
编　者　陈丽娇　高　枫　田昊宇
　　　　瞿晶磊　刘　青　张爱莲
　　　　郭丽丽　石　榴

清华大学出版社
北京

内 容 简 介

本书旨在帮助学习者全面了解英语公共演讲及有效沟通所必需的实践技能，包括精彩的演讲音频、演讲摘录等内容，既能展示世界各国著名演讲者的风采，又能使学习者接触到公共演讲的最佳范例。此外，本书有针对性地设计了一系列演讲任务，旨在强化学习者将演讲音频、演讲范例和技巧理论环节中学到的知识应用于实践的能力。

本书适合普通高校修读相关课程的本科生和研究生，以及致力于提升公共演讲能力的大众读者使用。

版权所有，侵权必究。举报：010-62782989，beiqinquan@tup.tsinghua.edu.cn。

图书在版编目（CIP）数据

英语公众演讲进阶教程 / 赵玲总主编；谢晓梅，刘莹，鲁亚侠主编.
北京：清华大学出版社，2024.9. --（高校英语选修课系列教材）. -- ISBN 978-7-302-67265-4
Ⅰ.H311.9
中国国家版本馆 CIP 数据核字第 2024EQ8143 号

责任编辑：杨文娟
封面设计：子　一
责任校对：王荣静
责任印制：宋　林

出版发行：清华大学出版社
网　　址：https://www.tup.com.cn，https://www.wqxuetang.com
地　　址：北京清华大学学研大厦 A 座　　　邮　编：100084
社 总 机：010-83470000　　　　　　　　　邮　购：010-62786544
投稿与读者服务：010-62776969，c-service@tup.tsinghua.edu.cn
质量反馈：010-62772015，zhiliang@tup.tsinghua.edu.cn
印 装 者：北京同文印刷有限责任公司
经　　销：全国新华书店
开　　本：185mm×260mm　　　印　张：14　　　字　数：336 千字
版　　次：2024 年 11 月第 1 版　　　　　　　印　次：2024 年 11 月第 1 次印刷
定　　价：62.00 元

产品编号：096555-01

Preface

Mastering English Public Speaking: A Progressive Approach is a versatile and comprehensive resource, designed to offer both theoretical knowledge and practical skills. This coursebook is tailored to aid language learners in mastering the fundamental theories of rhetoric while also cultivating practical public speaking abilities.

Within its pages, this coursebook presents an extensive range of learning materials, including the principles of effective public speaking, speech excerpts, and audios of some famous sample speeches. The aim of this coursebook is to guide learners through a gradual exploration of the art of public speaking, starting from the very basics and progressing to the delivery of speeches for special occasions.

This coursebook covering major aspects of speech preparation and presentation is divided into twelve units. Each unit incorporates various learning activities, such as listening, reading, writing, and speaking. These activities are meticulously designed based on a product-oriented approach, aiming to equip language learners with the skills needed to excel in public speaking.

In each unit, we commence with the presentation of a renowned speech as a listening material, allowing learners to immerse themselves in a model public speech. Subsequently, a classic public speech manuscript is provided, offering insights into the art of composing a speech. Then the speech analysis that follows deepens learners' understanding of the principles of effective public speaking, both in theory and in practice.

The Skill Focus section of each unit provides a comprehensive overview of the theoretical aspects of public speaking, followed by a series of exercises designed to reinforce learners' understanding. These exercises include true or false statements, multiple choice questions, and speech writing prompts, ensuring that learners develop a strong grasp of public speaking techniques. The Skill Focus section is then complemented by a speaking task, which encourages learners to apply their new found knowledge to topic selection, speech preparation, and delivery. To facilitate continuous improvement, learners are provided with public speech rubrics to evaluate their own speeches as well as those of their peers.

This coursebook stands out with its unique features such as audio recordings with QR codes in the listening exercises. This allows learners to easily consolidate and improve their public speaking skills. Additionally, all questions have answers available in the online workbook, enabling learners to review and reinforce their learning after each unit.

This coursebook is dedicated to improving speaking progress through ample public speaking practice. We highly recommend this resource to anyone seeking to gain profound insights into the art of public speaking, whether from a theoretical perspective or for practical applications in their studies, careers, or daily life.

We sincerely hope that you enjoy using this coursebook and that it leads you to success in your public speaking endeavor.

Authors
August 17, 2024

Contents

Unit 1   **Speaking Confidently and Ethically 1**

1.1 Speech Reading: Why Study Public Speaking? 2
1.2 Skill Focus: Speaking Confidently and Ethically 8
    1.2.1 The Basics of Public Speaking 8
    1.2.2 Speaking Confidently 11
    1.2.3 Speaking Ethically 11
1.3 Speaking Task: Making the First Introductory Speech 15
1.4 Self-Reflection: Evaluating Your Speech on Speaking Confidently and Ethically 15

Unit 2   **Analyzing the Audience 19**

2.1 Speech Reading: Gettysburg Address 20
2.2 Skill Focus: Analyzing the Audience 23
    2.2.1 Importance of Audience Analysis 23
    2.2.2 Audience Analysis 24
    2.2.3 Getting Information About the Audience 26
    2.2.4 Audience Adaptation 27
2.3 Speaking Task: Making a Speech After Audience Analysis 32
2.4 Self-Reflection: Audience Analysis and Adaptation 32

Unit 3   **Selecting a Topic and a Purpose 35**

3.1 Speech Reading: Day of Infamy 36

3.2 Skill Focus: Selecting a Topic and a Purpose 40
    3.2.1 Selecting a Topic 40
    3.2.2 Selecting a Purpose 40
    3.2.3 Drafting a Central Idea 44
    3.2.4 Drafting the Main Points 45
3.3 Speaking Task: Make a Speech Developed from a Topic 49
3.4 Self-Reflection: Evaluating the Specific Purpose and the Central Idea Statements 50

Unit 4 Organizing a Speech 51

4.1 Speech Reading: Stay Hungry, Stay Foolish 52
4.2 Skill Focus: Organizing a Speech 56
    4.2.1 Chronological Pattern 56
    4.2.2 Spatial Pattern 58
    4.2.3 Topical Pattern 59
    4.2.4 Causal Pattern and Effect Pattern 60
4.3 Speaking Task: Making a Speech About Ren in Confucianism 66
4.4 Self-Reflection: Evaluating the Organization of Your Speech 67

Unit 5 Opening and Closing of a Speech 69

5.1 Speech Reading: A Personal Journey and a Call to Action for a Paid Parental Leave 70
5.2 Skill Focus: Opening and Closing of a Speech 74
    5.2.1 Opening of a Speech 74
    5.2.2 Closing of a Speech 78
5.3 Speaking Task: Making a Speech on an Unforgettable Person 83
5.4 Self-Reflection: Evaluating the Opening and Closing of Your Speech 83

Unit 6 Speaking to Inform 85

6.1 Speech Reading: The Chinese Dream of the Great Renewal 86
6.2 Skill Focus: Speaking to Inform 90

		6.2.1	Choosing a Focused Informative Speech Topic.......................90
		6.2.2	Avoiding Faux or Fake Informative Speech Topics.................91
		6.2.3	Writing an Informative Speech Outline 92
	6.3	Speaking Task: Making an Informative Speech About ChatGPT 99	
	6.4	Self-Reflection: Evaluating Your Informative Speech.......................100	

Unit 7 Speaking to Persuade..103

7.1	Speech Reading: Yes, We Can 104	
7.2	Skill Focus: Speaking to Persuade..109	
	7.2.1	Persuasion 109
	7.2.2	Target Audience..110
	7.2.3	Different Types of Questions 110
	7.2.4	Organization Based on Types of Persuasive Speeches............112
	7.2.5	Methods of Persuation..117
	7.2.6	Fallacy 124
7.3	Speaking Task: Making a Persuasive Speech 130	
7.4	Self-Reflection: Evaluating Your Persuasive Speech 130	

Unit 8 Using Language Effectively 133

8.1	Speech Reading: I Have a Dream..134	
8.2	Skill Focus: Using Language Effectively..138	
	8.2.1	Being Concrete 138
	8.2.2	Being Precise..139
	8.2.3	Being Inclusive 140
	8.2.4	Being Familiar 141
	8.2.5	Being Rhetorical 141
8.3	Speaking Task: Delivering the Opening Address at a Conference.....143	
8.4	Self-Reflection: Evaluating Your Opening Address............................144	

Unit 9 Supporting Your Ideas 147

9.1	Speech Reading: We Shall Fight on the Beaches...............................148
9.2	Skill Focus: Supporting Your Ideas..154

		9.2.1 Supporting Materials 154
		9.2.2 Types of Supporting Materials 155
9.3	Speaking Task: Introducing Chinese Architecture 162
9.4	Self-Reflection: Evaluating the Supporting Materials of Your Speech 162

Unit 10 Using Visual Aids Effectively 165

10.1	Speech Reading: Transcending Boundaries 166
10.2	Skill Focus: Using Visual Aids Effectively.. 171
	10.2.1 Kinds of Visual Aids.. 171
	10.2.2 Preparing Presentation Aids... 175
	10.2.3 Presenting Visual Aids.. 176
10.3	Speaking Task: Making a Speech with Visual Aids............................ 179
10.4	Self-Reflection: Evaluating Your Speech in Using Visual Aids 179

Unit 11 Talking to Your Audience 181

11.1	Speech Reading: Education for Sustainable Development 182
11.2	Skill Focus: Talking to Your Audience.. 185
	11.2.1 Delivery Style.. 186
	11.2.2 Non-verbal Strategies 187
	11.2.3 Online Speech Delivery 189
11.3	Speaking Task: Running for the President of the Student Union 195
11.4	Self-Reflection: Evaluating a Presentation in Talking to the Audience 195

Unit 12 Speaking on Special Occasions 197

12.1	Speech Reading: The Tragedy of the Challenger Crew 198
12.2	Skill Focus: Types of and Principles for Special Occasion Speeches 202
	12.2.1 Speech of Introduction 202
	12.2.2 Speech of Presentation 203

	12.2.3	Speech of Acceptance 204
	12.2.4	Toast 204
	12.2.5	Commemorative Speech 205
12.3	**Speaking Task: Making a Speech on a Special Occasion 209**
12.4	**Self-Reflection: Evaluating Your Special Occasion Speech 210**

Unit 1

Speaking Confidently and Ethically

In this unit you will learn to:

- define the importance of public speaking;
- know the basic mode of speech communication process;
- explain the reasons for stage fright;
- apply strategies to deal with stage fright;
- get familiar with the guidelines for ethical speaking;
- deliver the first introductory speech confidently and ethically.

 ## 1.1 Speech Reading: Why Study Public Speaking?

Activity 1 Lead-in Listening

Listen to the speech and answer the following questions.

1. Do you think the champion speaker did a very good job in terms of speech content, organization, language, and delivery? Why or why not?

2. What is the symbol of China in your eyes?

3. In what order did the champion speaker organize her speech?

Activity 2 Pre-reading Questions

1. Why do you decide to take the Public Speaking course in this term?

2. Have you ever delivered a satisfactory public speech?

4. How did you feel before, during, and after your speech?

5. How do you evaluate your speech?

6. What are the major benefits of public speaking?

Unit 1　Speaking Confidently and Ethically

Why Study Public Speaking?[1]

1　Today, beyond the relative security of the college or university classroom, nearly 7,000 speakers will stand in front of the American audience and deliver speeches. And during those same twenty-four hours, people will make more than 30 million business presentations. These speakers will express and **elaborate their ideas**, **champion the clause**, and promote their products or services. Those who are successful will make sales, obtain support, and educate and entertain their listeners. Many will enhance their reputations as effective speakers. To achieve these goals, each will be using the skills, principles, and arts of public speaking.

2　Consider, too, that somewhere on a college campus right now is the student who will one day deliver an **inaugural address** after being sworn in as president of the United States; the student who will appear on national television to accept the Tony Award[①] for Best Actress, or the Academy Award[②] for Best Director; and the student who will present breakthrough medical research findings to a national conference of doctors and medical technicians, or whose words will announce the passage of important legislation.

3　Studying and practicing public speaking benefit you personally, professionally, and publicly.

Personal Benefits of Studying Public Speaking

4　First, mastering public speaking can help you to acquire skills important to your success in college. According to a recent Carnegie Foundation report:

*To succeed in college, undergraduates should be able to write and speak with clarity, and to read and listen with comprehension. Language and thought are **inextricably** connected, and as undergraduates develop their linguistic skills, they improve the quality of their thinking and become intellectually and socially **empowered**.*

5　Second, public speaking can help you to become more knowledgeable. There is a saying that we learn: 10 percent of what we read, 10 percent of what we hear, 10 percent of what we see, and 70 percent of what we speak.

6　Consider for a moment two different ways of studying lecture notes for an exam. One method is to read and reread your note silently. An alternative is more active and makes you a sender of messages. You stand in your room, put your lecture notes on your dresser, and deliver the lecture out loud, pretending you are the instructor explaining the material to the class. Which method do you think promotes better

---

[1] This text is adapted from *New College English* (Book 5, 2nd ed.), Beijing: Foreign Language Teaching and Research Press.

understanding and retention of the course material? You will not be surprised to learn that it's the second method.

7   Speaking is an active process. You discover ideas, shape them into a message, and deliver that message using your voice and body. The act of speaking is a crucial set of your thinking skills. As the British author E. M. Forster observed, "How do I know what I think until I've seen what I've said?" The process of developing and delivering an idea clarifies it and helps it uniquely your own.

Professional Benefits of Studying Public Speaking

8   Studying communication, especially public speaking, is important to you not only personally but also professionally. In fact, numerous studies document a strong relationship between communication competence and career success. Effective speaking skills enhance your chances of first securing employment and then advancing in your career. Hafer and Hoth surveyed thirty-seven companies, asking them to rate the characteristics they considered most important when hiring an employee. Out of twenty-six characteristics, oral communication skills ranked first.

9   More recently, three speech and business professors collected 428 responses from personnel managers in business organizations to determine the "factors most important in helping graduating college students to obtain employment". Oral communication skills ranked first and listening second. The researchers concluded:

> *From the results of this study, it appears that the skills most valued in the contemporary job market are communication skills. The skills of oral communication (both interpersonal and public), listening, written communication, and the trait of enthusiasm are seen as the most important. It would appear to follow that university officials wishing to be of the greatest help to their graduates in finding employment should make sure that basic competencies in oral and written communication are developed. Courses in listening, interpersonal, and public communication would form the basis of meeting the oral communication competencies.*

10   Once you are hired, your speaking skills continue to work for you, becoming your ticket to career success and advancement. Researchers Roger Mosvick and Robert Nelson found that managers and technical professionals spend approximately twice as much time speaking and listening as they do reading and writing. A survey of 500 executives found that speaking skills "rated second only to job knowledge as important factors in a businessperson's success". That same study also showed that effective communication helped to improve company productivity and understanding among employees. Oral communication and public speaking clearly play a critical role in your professional life.

Public Benefits of Studying Public Speaking

11 Finally, public speaking can help you to play your role as a member of society. As the German writer Thomas Mann noted, "Speech is civilization itself. The word, even the most **contradictory** word, preserves **contact**—it is silence which isolates." Public speaking is an important part of creating a society of informed and active citizens.

12 A democratic society is shaped, in part, by the **eloquence** of its leaders:

—Franklin Roosevelt, who rallied a nation during the Great Depression[3] by declaring, "The only thing we have to fear is fear itself";

—John F. Kennedy, who urged citizen involvement, **exhorting us to** "Ask not what your country can do for you; ask what you can do for your country";

—Martin Luther King, Jr., who challenged us to dream of a day when people will be judged not "by the color of their skin but by the content of their character".

13 But a democratic society is also shaped by the quiet eloquence of everyday citizens:

—the police officer who **informs** residents of a crime-plagued area how to set up a neighborhood watch program;

—the social worker who addresses the city council and secures funding for a sale house for abused and runaway children;

—the elementary school teacher who speaks to civic clubs, generating support for a meals-on-wheels program for elderly citizens **confined** to their homes.

14 In each of these instances, the speaker used the power of the spoken words to address a need and **solicit** an appropriate audience response.

Analysis

The presenter delivers the speech in order to help college students to get a better understanding of the importance of public speaking and encourage them to study the art of public speaking for a brighter future. Of course, by using some public speaking skills, the presenter successfully achieves the goal.

Firstly, the speech is well-organized with a three-part anatomy—introduction, body, and conclusion. In the introduction part, the presenter makes a list of domains where public speaking is frequently made in order to relate the speech topic to the audience. By doing so, the presenter can get the audience's interest in the speech topic and engage them in thinking about the topic.

Besides, at the end of the introduction part, the presenter formulates a very solid central idea with "Studying and practicing public speaking benefit you personally, professionally, and publicly.". Therefore, the audience are navigated into understanding the personal, professional, and public benefits of public speaking.

Throughout the whole speech, the presenter uses examples, statistics, and testimony to support the main idea, which makes the speech credible and persuasive enough for the audience to understand the benefits of public speaking.

The presenter uses some brief and hypothetical examples to illustrate the importance of public speaking. For example, giving presentation on the lecture note during the final week is much more efficient than reciting the materials by oneself to prove that public speaking is personally beneficial to college students. Besides, the presenter also uses some very influential people as examples to prove that public speaking is socially beneficial to people.

In the speech, the presenter employs some statistics to make the speech more credible. For example, the presenter uses such statistics as "we learn: 10 percent of what we read, 10 percent of what we hear, 10 percent of what we see, and 70 percent of what we speak" to support the main point that "public speaking can help you to become more knowledgeable".

In addition to the use of examples and statistics, the presenter also uses testimony to make the speech more reliable. For example, the presenter uses "Speech is civilization itself. The word, even the most contradictory word, preserves contact—it is silence which isolates." to support the idea that public speaking is an important means of creating a society of informed and active citizens.

In the conclusion part, the presenter reinforces the central idea that "the speaker used the power of the spoken words to address a need and solicit an appropriate audience response" to highlight the importance of public speaking and signal the end of the speech.

In summary, the presenter successfully helps the audience to realize the importance of public speaking with a strong central idea, a clear and precise organizational pattern, and adequate evidence including examples, statistics, and testimony to support the main idea.

Useful Words & Expressions

confine	v.	控制，限制
contact	n.	联络用的
contradictory	adj.	矛盾的，对立的
eloquence	n.	能言善辩
empower	v.	授予……权力
inextricably	adv.	密不可分地，解不开地
solicit	v.	征求，募集

champion the clause	支持条款
elaborate one's ideas	详尽阐述某人的想法
exhort sb. to do sth.	劝告某人做某事
inaugural address	就职演讲
inform sb. of sth.	通知某人某事

Notes

① the Tony Award: Established in 1947, it is the highest award for American plays and musicals, jointly established by the Broadway League and the American Theater Wing. It is known alongside the Oscars for film, the Grammy Awards for music, and the Emmy Awards for television as one of the four top awards in the American arts.

② the Academy Award: It is a film award hosted by the Academy of Motion Picture Arts and Sciences, established in 1929. This award is the oldest, most authoritative, and professional film award in American history and is also the most influential film award worldwide.

③ the Great Depression: It originated in the United States between 1929 and 1933, and later spread to the entire capitalist world, including economic crises in capitalist countries such as the British Empire, the Third French Republic, Germany, and the Empire of Japan. It was characterized by its long duration, wide range, and strong destructive power.

Critical Thinking

1. How does understanding the speech communication process enhance one's ability to speak confidently and ethically?

2. What role does intercultural communicative competence play in public speaking, and how can it be developed for more effective cross-cultural communication?

3. How does public speaking differ from conversation, and what adjustments can speakers make to use them effectively?

4. How can public speakers ensure that their speeches are not only effective but also responsible and respectful?

5. How does critical thinking enhance the ethical dimensions of public speaking?

1.2 Skill Focus: Speaking Confidently and Ethically

Public speaking is an essential skill that involves effective communication with a group of people through words, physical delivery, and sometimes visual or audio aids. It can be intimidating for many individuals, but it is a skill that can be developed and improved over time. To speak confidently and ethically, it is important for you to understand the speech communication process, intercultural communicative competence, critical thinking, and how public speaking differs from conversation. By applying these principles to practice, you can become a more effective and confident public speaker.

1.2.1 The Basics of Public Speaking

Public speaking is an art, but not a talent. In order to improve your public speaking skills, you should know some basics about public speaking, such as the speech communication process, intercultural communicative competence, critical thinking, the similarities and differences between public speaking and conversation, and speaking in a multicultural world. Based on your understanding of the basics of public speaking, you should put the following tips into practice to speak in public confidently and ethically.

1. Speech Communication Process

Regardless of the different kinds of speech communication involved, seven elements in a speech communication process should be taken into consideration, which are situation, speaker, channel, message, audience, interference, and feedback.

> **Examples**
>
> (1) Situation
>
> It was 5:15 p.m., and the Midwest Food Festival and Expo had been going on all day. Gourmet food vendors from the Great Lakes region were presenting their products to distributors and restaurant owners, but the presentations had taken much longer than expected.

Unit 1　Speaking Confidently and Ethically

(2) Speaker

　　Jason Cruz, the owner and operator of a gourmet salsa company, was worried. As the last speaker of the day, he knew he faced a tough situation. He had been allotted 30 minutes, but the festival was scheduled to end in 15 minutes and the success of his products depended in large part on his presentation.

(3) Channel

　　Jason stepped to the microphone and began to speak. He could see members of the audience looking at their watches, and he knew they were eager to have dinner after a long day of meeting.

(4) Message

　　Now that he had the audience's attention, Jason presented each of his products as briefly as he could. He streamlined his planned remarks to emphasize the salsa that would be the most appealing to grocery shoppers and restaurant diners. He ended by handing out samples of two pieces of new salsa that had won awards in recent food shows.

(5) Audience

　　The audience were grocery shoppers and restaurant diners, who were eager to have dinner after a day's meeting.

(6) Interference

　　"Good afternoon," Jason said, "and thanks for your attention. I know everyone is ready to relax after a long day. So am I. I was given 30 minutes to tell you about my salsa, but I'll do my best to finish in 15 minutes. I think you'll find the time well worth your while, because your customers are going to love my products." Jason was relieved to see people smiling as they settled back in their seats.

(7) Feedback

　　As promised, Jason finished in 15 minutes. "So, that's it!" he concluded. "Thanks for your attention after such a long day." The festival organizer came up to Jason after his presentation. "Great stuff—both the talk and the salsa," she said. "Next year I think we'll try to make all the presentations as concise and efficient as yours."

2. Public Speaking and Cultural Diversity

　　Speech making is becoming more and more complex as cultural diversity increases, and part of the complexity stems from the differences in language from culture to culture, so you should develop the ability to communicate effectively in cross-cultural situations. When talking to the cross-cultural audience, you must be especially alert to how cultural factors will affect their responses to your speech. You should show respect for the cultural values and expectations of the audience. But some inexperienced public speakers sometimes fail to take their audience's cultural values and customs into consideration due to ethnocentrism.

Ethnocentrism can play a positive role in creating group pride and loyalty. But it can also lead to prejudice and hostility toward different racial, ethnic, religious, or cultural groups. To be an effective public speaker in a multicultural world, you need to have intercultural communicative competence and keep in mind that all people have their special beliefs and customs, so you should try to avoid ethnocentrism.

Avoiding ethnocentrism does not mean that you must agree with the values and practices of all groups and cultures. At times you might try to convince people of different cultures to change their traditional ways of doing.

Due to the diversity of the modern world, in which people have different cultural backgrounds, you should be alert to how cultural factors might affect how the audience respond and adapt your message accordingly when you work on your speeches.

3. Public Speaking and Critical Thinking

Certainly, demonstrating respect for cultural diversity does not imply that you should undervalue your own culture. As an ethical speaker, you should cultivate your critical thinking skills.

Critical thinking involves the ability to think clearly and systematically about various aspects of an issue, such as the logical connections between ideas, the validity of evidence, and the distinction between facts and opinions. Critical thinking is a skill that can help you to further develop your arguments and position your speech in a strong manner. It utilizes your thought, plan, and action. You should be sure to consider the research at-hand and develop an argument that is logical and connects to the audience.

Critical thinking has been regarded as a vitally important part of public speaking because it can enhance your skills as a critical thinker in many occasions. For example, when you plan the structure of your speeches, when you organize your thoughts logically and cohesively, or when you express your ideas in clear and accurate language, critical thinking can help you to think clearly, accurately, and effectively.

4. Public Speaking and Conversation

To get a better understanding of the nature of public speaking, you should be aware of the similarities and differences between public speaking and conversation. There are some similarities between public speaking and conversation: (1) organizing your thoughts logically; (2) tailoring your message to the audience; (3) telling a story for the maximum impact; (4) adapting to the audience's feedback.

Compared with conversation, public speaking is more highly structured and requires more formal language and a different method of delivery.

1.2.2 Speaking Confidently

Public speaking is important in both personal and professional life, but there are indications that public speaking ranks high among the things that people fear the most. For most people, when they speak they are very nervous or stage frightened. When delivering a speech, you should pay attention to the importance of speaking confidently.

Speaking with confidence has great personal and professional benefits, such as building self-esteem, building trust and relationships with people around them, and having open discussions with others.

However, stage fright, which is one of the barriers to prevent you from speaking confidently, is a common phenomenon that cuts across language, culture, and national borders. Speaking in public is very challenging for all of you, so you should gain some knowledge about speaking confidently by exploring what stage fright is, examining the different causes of nervousness, and using some strategies to manage your fears of public speaking.

Here are some tips on dealing with the nervousness: (1) practice more; (2) prepare, prepare and prepare; (3) think positively; (4) use the help of visualization; (5) know the fact that most nervousness is not visible; (6) don't expect perfection, etc.

Only after you know that stage fright is quite normal to all public speakers can you deal with nervousness positively, and then become more confident in public speaking and in other areas of your life and work.

1.2.3 Speaking Ethically

Public speaking is a way of making your ideas public, a way of sharing your ideas with other people, a way of influencing other people, and a form of empowerment. It carries heavy ethical responsibilities. Therefore, you should be ethical to take responsibility for whatever you say in your speech. Speaking with ethics is very important because it can enhance human worth and dignity by fostering truthfulness, fairness, responsibility, personal integrity, and respect.

As for ethics, it is the branch of philosophy that deals with issues of right or wrong human affairs. There are two most important aspects in ethical speaking: remaining honest while avoiding plagiarism, and setting and meeting the speech goals.

Plagiarism means presenting another person's language or ideas as one's own. There are three kinds of plagiarism: global plagiarism, patchwork plagiarism, and incremental plagiarism. Global plagiarism means using the content of a speech entirely from a single source and passing it off as one's own. Patchwork plagiarism is the one using ideas or language from two or three sources and passing them off as one's own. Incremental plagiarism means failing to give credit for particular parts of a speech, which are borrowed from other people. It always occurs when a speaker fails to give credit for specific quotations and paraphrases that are borrowed from other people.

Ethical speaking means speaking in a manner that is clear, concise, truthful, and responsible. As a speaker, you should try your best to achieve the speech goals and be truthful and devoted to the good of society. In order to speak ethically, you can follow the following basic guidelines: (1) make sure your goals are ethically sound; (2) be fully prepared for each speech and be honest in what you say; (3) avoid name-calling and other forms of abusive language; (4) put ethical principles into practice.

To be an ethical speaker, you should set a sound goal of your speech, do a thorough research of the topic, use statistics, testimony, and other evidence accurately and fairly, be free of plagiarism, and make good preparation for the upcoming speeches, making assuring that you can achieve the desired speech goals.

Exercises

I. **Decide whether the following statements are TRUE (T), FALSE (F) or NOT GIVEN (NG) according to the Skill Focus in this unit.**

1. English public speaking skills are crucial to your personal success as you work and live in a world shaped by globalization. (   )

2. In order to be a successful public speaker, you must have your personal credibility, the knowledge of the subject, the preparation of the speech, the manner of speaking, and the sensibility to the audience and the occasion. (   )

3. The audience's frame of reference does not play a very important part while interpreting the message delivered by the speaker. (   )

Unit 1　Speaking Confidently and Ethically

4. Public speaking and ordinary conversation are similar in that both involve adapting to The audience's feedback. (　)

5. Speech making becomes much easier as cultural diversity increases. (　)

6. Regardless of your topic, your speech should have three main parts—an introduction, a body, and a conclusion. (　)

7. The larger your audience is, the more formal your presentation must be. (　)

8. Having a higher expectation of your public speech will help to reduce stage fright. (　)

9. Preparation is a very effective way to reduce stage fright. It is estimated that proper preparation can reduce stage fright by up to 75%. (　)

10. Avoiding ethnocentrism means that you must agree with the values and practices of all groups and cultures. (　)

II. Choose the best options to answer the following questions or fill in the blanks according to the information given in this unit.

1. Speech making is a form of power, so you should always be sure to speak _____.
   A. concisely   B. persuasively
   C. ethically   D. consistently

2. As a public speaker, you should face ethical issues when _____.
   A. selecting the topic for your speech
   B. researching your speech
   C. organizing your speech
   D. all of the above

3. What are the major reasons for being nervous while making a speech to the audience?
   A. The lack of self-confidence.
   B. The higher expectation to be perfect.
   C. Enough preparation for the speech.
   D. Only A and B.

4. _____ is the belief that one's own group or culture is superior to all the other groups or cultures.
   A. Ego-centrism   B. Ethnocentrism
   C. Elitism   D. Patriotism

5. Stealing ideas or language from two or three sources and passing them off as one's own are called _____.
   A. global plagiarism
   B. patchwork plagiarism
   C. incremental plagiarism
   D. ethnocentrism

6. Which of the following is NOT one of the guidelines for ethical speechmaking?
   A. Be honest with what you say.
   B. Avoid name-calling and other forms of abusive language.
   C. Make sure your goals are ethically sound.
   D. Explain your credibility on the topic at the very beginning of your speech.

7. When you prepare your first ice-breaker speech, how will you organize your speech?
   A. Get the attention and interest of your audience in the introduction part.
   B. Use chronological or topic order to organize the body part.
   C. Make your audience know that you are going to finish and reinforce your major theme in the conclusion part.
   D. All of the above.

8. Rather than trying to eliminate stage fright, you should aim at transforming it into _____.
   A. confident apprehension
   B. professional stage fright
   C. positive nervousness
   D. shared anxiety

9. The primary purpose of speech making is to _____.
   A. gain a desired response from the audience
   B. display your knowledge about a topic
   C. enhance the audience's self-concept
   D. promote your ethical standards

10. The tendency of people to be concerned about all with their own values, beliefs, and well-being is called _____.
    A. ego-centrism
    B. ethnocentrism
    C. individualism
    D. plagiarism

1.3 Speaking Task: Making the First Introductory Speech

Task I Introduce yourself / your classmate / a guest speaker to your classmates with at least 300 words and then deliver the speech to your classmates.

Your speech should be in an organic structure with an introduction, a body and a conclusion, and it can cover the following six aspects: (1) name; (2) introduction of yourself / your classmate / guest speaker; (3) background—family background and educational background; (4) personality, interest, passion and goal; (5) personal details appropriate to the setting of the speech; (6) unity.

Task II Deliver a speech introducing the most successful person in your eyes with at least 300 words to your classmates.

The following are some tips for your reference: (1) speech must have an introduction, a body, and a conclusion; (2) speak extemporaneously with brief notes, but not a manuscript; (3) practice your speech confidently and ethically at least 3–5 times in front of a mirror or recording device before your presentation; (4) use verbal language and non-verbal language; (5) make sure that your speech should conform to the time limit (3 minutes).

1.4 Self-Reflection: Evaluating Your Speech on Speaking Confidently and Ethically

Evaluate your speech on speaking confidently and ethically based on the rubrics provided. Rate your speech on each point: E—excellent, G—good, A—average, F—fair, P—poor.

Checklist: Speaking Confidently and Ethically

Items	Scores					Comments
	E	G	A	F	P	
Are you enthusiastic about your speech topic?						
Have you thoroughly developed the content of your speech?						
Have you worked on the introduction so your speech will get off to a good start?						
Have you rehearsed your speech orally until you are confident about its delivery?						
Have you worked on turning negative thoughts about your speech into positive ones?						
Do you realize that nervousness is normal, even among experienced speakers?						
Do you understand that much nervousness is not visible to the audience?						
Are you focused on communicating with your audience, rather than on worrying about your nervousness?						
Have you visualized yourself speaking confidently and getting a positive response from the audience?						
Have you examined your goals to make sure they are ethically sound?						
Have you fulfilled your ethical obligation to fully prepare for the speech? (1) Have you done a thorough job of studying and researching the topic? (2) Have you prepared diligently so as not to deliver misleading information?						

(To be continued)

Unit 1 Speaking Confidently and Ethically

(Continued)

Items	Scores					Comments
	E	G	A	F	P	
Is your speech free of plagiarism? (1) Can you vouch that the speech represents your own work, your own thinking, and your own language? (2) Do you cite the sources of all quotations and paraphrases?						
Are you honest in what you say in the speech? (1) Is the speech free of any false or deliberately deceptive statements? (2) Does the speech present statistics, testimony, and other kinds of evidence fairly and accurately?						
Have you made a conscious effort to put ethical principles into practice in preparing your speech?						

Unit 2

Analyzing the Audience

In this unit you will learn to:

- realize the importance of audience analysis;
- analyze the psychology of audience;
- get information about the audience;
- adapt the speech to the specific audience.

 ## 2.1 Speech Reading: Gettysburg Address

Activity 1 Lead-in Listening

Listen to the speech and answer the following questions.

1. When should you do audience analysis if you are going to give a public speech?

2. What are the three main things that you need to consider when you analyze the audience before the speech?

3. In what ways can you find out who your audience is?

Activity 2 Pre-reading Questions

1. How much do you know about Abraham Lincoln?

2. Why is Abraham Lincoln's Gettysburg Address considered one of the most significant speeches in American history?

Gettysburg Address[1]

1   Four **score** and seven years ago our fathers brought forth on this continent, a new nation, **conceived** in Liberty, and **dedicated to** the **proposition** that all men

---

[1] This text is adapted from Abraham Lincoln's Gettysburg Address from the Owleyes website.

are created equal.

2   Now we are engaged in a great civil war①, testing whether that nation, or any nation so conceived and so dedicated, can long **endure**. We are met on a great battle-field of that war. We have come to dedicate a portion of that field, as a final resting place for those who here gave their lives that that nation might live. It is altogether **fitting** and proper that we should do this.

3   But, in a larger sense, we can not dedicate—we can not **consecrate**—we can not **hallow** this ground. The brave men, living and dead, who struggled here, have consecrated it far above our poor power to add or **detract**. The world will little note, nor long remember what we say here, but it can never forget what they did here. It is for us the living, rather, to be dedicated here to the unfinished work which they who fought here have thus far so nobly advanced. It is rather for us to be here dedicated to the great task remaining before us; that from these honored dead we take increased devotion to that cause for which they gave the last full measure of devotion; that we here highly resolve that these dead shall not have died **in vain**; that this nation, under God, shall have a new birth of freedom; and that government of the people, by the people, for the people, shall not perish from the earth.

Analysis

Lincoln's Gettysburg Address is very brief with only 272 words, but it's acclaimed as one of the most significant speeches. It is a very powerful speech which emphasizes unity, equality, and democracy. The purpose of Lincoln's Gettysburg Address is to inspire the audience to honor the sacrifices for freedom and to continue the fight for a united nation.

In order to achieve the goal, Lincoln uses testimony as evidence to support his idea in the speech. For example, at the very beginning, he quotes both the Bible and the Declaration of Independence to signal that the audience should trust his words if they trust the words in those documents. When trying to persuade the audience into supporting him, he seeks out principles and anchors the arguments from that solid foundation, which makes his speech quite credible.

Besides, Lincoln employs such classic rhetorical devices as triad, contrast, and repetition to transform his words from bland to poetic.

The first rhetorical device used in the speech is triad, which can make his speech poetic and memorable. He uses the following two famous triads, "we can not dedicate, we can not consecrate, we can not hallow this ground" and "government of the people, by the people, for the people", which are passed down from generation to generation.

The second rhetorical device used in the speech is contrast. He uses contrast in order to inspire the audience to fight for freedom, liberty, and equality. For example, "… for those who here gave their lives that that nation might live." Therefore, the death of the soldiers contrasts with the life of the nation, which is worth the audience's awe so they will be inspired by the speech to fight for the rights of American people. Similarly, "The world will little note, nor longer remember what we say here, but it can never forget what they did here." The sharp contrast is used to inspire the audience to make a difference.

The third rhetorical device used by Lincoln is the repetition of the most important words to lay focus on something. For example, the following words are repeated: "we" (10 times), "here" (8 times), "dedicate" (6 times), and "nation" (5 times). By the repetitive use of these words, Lincoln emphasizes his central point that all the audience must dedicate themselves to saving the united nation. The word "we" creates a bond with the audience (it's not about you or I, but it's about us together). The word "here" casts Gettysburg as the spring board to propel them forward. The word "dedicate" is more powerful than saying "we must try to do this" because "nation" gives the higher purpose.

Gettysburg Address begins with the founding of the nation and ends with the crossroad, so it's crucial that all the audience should choose the right way to fight against the enemies. In this way, the speech achieves its goal of inspiring the audience to fight for unity, equality, and democracy.

Useful Words & Expressions

conceive	v.	孕育；构思，构想
consecrate	v.	奉献；使神圣
detract	v.	转移，减去
endure	v.	忍受，忍耐；持续存在
fitting	adj.	合适的，恰当的
hallow	v.	把……奉为神圣
proposition	n.	提议，提案；观点
score	n.	二十；很多，大量
dedicate to		献身，贡献
in vain		徒劳无功地

Notes

a great civil war: It refers to the American Civil War, also known as the War between the states. It was the deadliest conflict in American history, fought between the Northern

United States, known as the United States of America, and the Southern Confederate States of America. The war began with the Confederate bombardment of Fort Sumter and ended with the victory of the Union in the North. The Civil War was the first large-scale war following the Industrial Revolution, during which modern standards for tactics, strategic thinking, and battlefield medicine were established. With 3.5 million people participating, the vast majority of whom were volunteers, the official count of war dead reached 620,000, a number exceeding the combined total of all other American wars.

Critical Thinking

1. How does considering the listeners, the occasion, and the speaker when selecting a topic contribute to the effectiveness of a speech?

2. What methods can be used to conduct audience analysis effectively? And how does this analysis influence the content and delivery of a speech?

3. In what ways can a speaker ensure that his or her speech meets the needs of the audience throughout the stages of public speaking?

4. How can a speaker balance his or her own interests and expertise with the audience's needs and expectations when selecting a speech topic?

5. In what ways does "Gettysburg Address" reflect the values and beliefs of the American people through the speech delivery?

2.2 Skill Focus: Analyzing the Audience

Before you determine the topic of your speech, you should take the target audience's needs into consideration and try your best to meet their needs at any stage of your public speaking. Therefore, it is of vital importance for you to do audience analysis before, in or even after the public speaking.

2.2.1 Importance of Audience Analysis

Audience analysis involves identifying the audience and adapting a speech to the audience's interests, level of understanding, attitudes, and beliefs. Taking an audience-centered approach is important because a speaker's effectiveness will be improved if the presentation is created and delivered in an appropriate manner.

Good public speakers are always audience-centered, and they try to gain a desired response from the audience and keep the audience foremost in mind at every stage of public speaking. But being audience-centered does not involve compromising your beliefs to get a favorable response. It means that you can remain true to yourself and speak ethically while adapting your message to the goals, values, and attitudes of your audience.

In order to achieve the goal of making a public speech, it is necessary for you to know the features of the audience, such as the audience's backgrounds and interests, their level of knowledge regarding the speech topic, and their attitudes towards your stance on the topic.

Audience analysis is the process of learning who your audience are, what they are thinking about, and how you can best reach them. Audience analysis, which can guide the stylistic and content choices you make for a presentation, is an essential step for you to make a public speech successfully.

Therefore, when working on your speeches, you should ask yourself three questions to be audience-centered: (1) to whom are you speaking? (2) what do you want them to know, believe, or do as a result of your speech? (3) what is the most effective way of composing and presenting your speech to accomplish the goal of your speech?

When audience analysis is conducted, you can acknowledge your audience and their beliefs, knowledge, and attitudes, which can guide you to select the topic that is relevant and useful to them. Controversial topics can be excellent, but you should be sure to consider your audience. What's more, you should consider cultural diversity, make your message clear, avoid offensive remarks, and speak with sincerity. Anyway, the more you know about your audience, the better your public speaking is likely to be.

2.2.2 Audience Analysis

Each speech contains two messages—one sent by the speaker and the other received by the audience. A message can be interpreted in different ways based on the audience's knowledge and experience. What you say is filtered through the audience's frame of reference—the sum of the audience's needs, interests, expectations, knowledge, experience, etc. In order to convey the intended messages successfully to the audience, you should take the factors of audience analysis into account all the way.

Generally, audience analysis mainly consists of demographic analysis, psychographic analysis, and situational analysis.

1. Demographic Analysis

Demographic analysis focuses on the demographic traits, such as age and gender, and takes audience diversity into consideration, such as educational background, religion, economic standing, ethic or cultural background, and the like. You may find clues about how your audience will respond to your speech by analyzing the demographic traits, which are beneficial.

Age is one of the most commonly considered demographic characteristics. Age can greatly impact a person's perspective, so you should be mindful of it when crafting a speech. For instance, ideas that may resonate with the younger audience may not be well-received by older ones. Gender is another common demographic characteristic that should be considered when crafting speeches. According to Deborah Tannen[1], a renowned linguistics scholar and author, men and women in the United States exhibit distinct communication styles. There are noticeable differences in how men and women communicate, as well as certain speech topics that may pique the interest of one gender over the other. It's essential to be mindful of the gender difference and avoid using language that could be perceived as sexist or discriminatory when delivering public speeches. By doing so, you can ensure that your message is received positively by all members of the audience.

As for the audience, it is a crucial aspect of audience analysis that goes beyond just considering racial and ethnic minorities. It's important to recognize that the audience can be diverse in many other ways as well, such as economic standing, and cultural background. Being mindful of the audience diversity means showing respect for all individuals and actively working to avoid making assumptions based on factors like racism, ethnocentrism, sexism, ageism, elitism, or any other form of bias.

While demographic analysis is valuable, it's essential to avoid stereotyping, which involves creating oversimplified images of particular groups of people. By doing so, you can ensure that your message is received positively by all the members of the audience and promote an inclusive and respectful environment.

---

1   Deborah Tannen. 2021. Three decades in the field of gender and language: A personal perspective. *Gender and Language, 15*(2): 232–241.

2. Psychographic Analysis

Psychographic analysis focuses on such things as values, opinions, attitudes, and beliefs. The audience's disposition toward you, toward the topic, and toward the occasion are crucial parts of the psychographic analysis.

The tendency of people to be concerned above all with their own values, beliefs, and well-being, which is called ego-centrism, makes audience analysis important to give a good speech.

3. Situational Analysis

Situational analysis consists of the audience size and the physical setting. No matter to what size group you are addressing, bear in mind the basic principle that the larger the audience, the more formal your presentation should be. Audience size may also affect your language, choice of appeals, and the use of visual aids. Physical setting generally includes time, room temperature, location of the lectern, and seating arrangements. Just remember to do what you can to control the influence of physical setting on your audience.

2.2.3 Getting Information About the Audience

In order to get information about the audience, there are three kinds of questions you can use to conduct an audience-analysis questionnaire, which are fixed-alternative questions, scale questions, and open-ended questions.

A fixed-alternative question offers a fixed choice between two or more responses.

> **Example**
>
> Are you a fan of TV reality shows?
> ☐ Yes.
> ☐ No.

A scale question resembles a fixed-alternative question, but it allows more leeway in responding.

> **Example**
>
> Do you agree or disagree with the following statement?
> Reality shows have improved the quality of TV programs.
> A. Strongly agree.

> B. Mildly agree.
>
> C. Undecided.
>
> D. Mildly disagree.
>
> E. Strongly disagree.

An open-ended question gives the maximum leeway in responding.

> **Example**
>
> What is the proper balance in TV programming between profits for the broadcasters and the cultural and moral enlightenment of the viewers?

Because each type of question has its own advantages and disadvantages, many questionnaires contain all the three types, through which you can elicit specific information about the audience and probe more deeply into the attitudes towards the speech topic. When designing your questionnaire, you should keep the following points in mind: (1) plan the questionnaire carefully to elicit precisely the information you need; (2) use all three types of questions; (3) make sure the questions are unambiguous; (4) keep the questionnaire brief.

Once you have completed the audience analysis, you can have a pretty clear picture of your audience, but this does not guarantee a successful speech. The keys are how well you use what you know in preparing and presenting the speech and how you adapt your speech to your audience.

2.2.4 Audience Adaptation

Once you complete the audience analysis, you must adapt your speech to make it clear and convincing, anticipate questions and objections, and try to answer them in advance.

1. Audience Adaptation Before the Speech

As you have seen, you must keep your audience in mind when making preparations. This involves more than simply remembering who your audience are. It also means firstly assessing how your audience is likely to respond to what you say in your speech, and secondly adjusting what you say to make it as clear, appropriate, and convincing as possible.

Try to imagine what they will like, what they will dislike, where they will have doubts or questions, whether they will need more details here or fewer there, and what will interest them and what will not. At every point, you must anticipate how your audience will respond to your speech.

2. Audience Adaptation During the Speech

No matter how hard you prepare, you may find there is always room for your adaptation. Maybe the audience will be much larger (or smaller) than you have anticipated, or the time for your speech has been reduced because the previous speaker has talked for too long.

If something like this happens to you, just adjust your delivery to the changed situations. And be sure to keep an eye out during your speech for audience feedback. If you find your audience frowning or responding with quizzical looks, you may need to back up and go over your point again.

3. Audience Adaptation After the Speech

After the speech, reflecting on your audience's response is an important part of the skill development. You should think after every speech about how the audience reacted and how you might modify the speech if you were to present it again. Keeping a journal of the speech, audience, and responses can help you to improve your public speaking skills a lot. Audience adaptation after the speech is an important part of preparing for your next presentation and an important part of becoming a more effective speaker in general.

The following is an audience adaptation worksheet which can be used when you prepare a speech.

Audience Adaptation Worksheet

1. What device(s) will you use in the introduction of your speech to gain the attention and interest of your audience?

   —Use a relevant and attention-grabbing quote or statistics related to the topic.

   —Share a personal story or experience that connects to the topic.

   —Ask a thought-provoking question that engages the audience.

   —Use humor or a surprising fact to pique the audience's interest.

2. What steps will you take in the introduction of your speech to relate the topic directly to your audience?

   —Explain why the topic is important and relevant to their lives.

—Connect the topic to current events or trends that they are familiar with.

—Share examples of how the topic has affected people in similar situations as your audience.

—Address any concerns or objections they may have about the topic of your speech.

3. What are the main points of the speech? Why do you plan to develop these particular main points for the audience?

—Identify the key ideas or arguments you want to convey in your speech.

—Explain why these main points are important and relevant to your audience.

—Consider any biases or perspectives your audience may hold and address them accordingly.

—Use examples, statistics, or anecdotes to support your main points.

4. Why have you selected the supporting materials for the audience?

—Choose materials that are relatable and familiar to your audience.

—Select examples or data that support your main points and resonate with your audience's values or experiences.

—Avoid using jargon or technical terms that may be unfamiliar to the audience.

—Ensure that your supporting materials are accurate, up-to-date, and reliable.

5. What steps have you taken to make your language clear and appropriate to the audience?

—Use simple and concise language that is easy for your audience to understand.

—Avoid using complex sentence structures or technical terms unless necessary.

—Use words and phrases that are familiar to your audience and avoid using slang or colloquialisms.

—Provide definitions or explanations for any specialized terms or concepts you use.

6. What adjustments will you make in the delivery rate of speech, volume, tone of voice, gestures, and the like to communicate your ideas to the audience?

—Adjust your speaking rate based on your audience's age, cultural background, and familiarity with the topic.

—Vary your volume and tone of voice to emphasize important points and maintain engagement.

—Use appropriate gestures and body language to enhance your message and convey enthusiasm.

—Be mindful of any cultural norms or expectations regarding non-verbal communication in your audience's context.

Exercises

I. Decide whether the following statements are TRUE (T), FALSE (F) or NOT GIVEN (NG) according to the Skill Focus in this unit.

1. The primary purpose of speechmaking is to gain a desired response from the audience. (   )

2. Being audience-centered involves compromising your beliefs to get a favorable response. (   )

3. When you face a speaking situation, do everything you can to control the influence of physical setting on your audience. (   )

4. There is very little diversity among the audience with similar demographic characteristics. (   )

5. Your audience's knowledge about your topic will determine what you can say in your speech. (   )

6. When putting together your own questionnaire, use all three types of questions: fixed-alternative questions, scale questions, and open-ended questions. (   )

7. The key to effective speaking is how well you use what you know in preparing and presenting the speech. (   )

8. You need to keep your audience in mind only during the speech. (   )

9. Some speakers keep a journal of their speeches, audience, and responses. (   )

10. "Do you think the one-child policy is a workable solution to the problem of food shortage in African countries?" is an example of an open-ended question. (   )

II. Choose the best options to answer the following questions or fill in the blanks according to the information given in this unit.

1. Good public speakers are _____.
   A. self-centered
   B. content-centered
   C. audience-centered
   D. delivery-centered

Unit 2   Analyzing the Audience

2. To be audience-centered, you need to keep all of the following questions in mind when you work on your speech EXCEPT _____.
   A. to whom you are speaking
   B. what you want them to know, believe, or do after your speech
   C. how you can justify using devious, unethical tactics to achieve your goal
   D. what the most effective way of composing and presenting your speech to accomplish that aim is

3. People don't usually expend the time and effort to attend a speech unless _____.
   A. they have some interest in the topic
   B. they are invited to the speech
   C. the speech is delivered by a celebrity
   D. attending the speech is a course requirement

4. Audience attitudes are the most important in _____ speeches.
   A. informative   B. persuasive
   C. commemorative   D. introductory

5. Which of the following questions is an open-ended question?
   A. Are you a fan of the TV reality show?
   B. What types of reality shows do you like best, science, dating, makeover, or documentary style?
   C. Why, in your opinion, are TV reality shows so popular?
   D. How many reality shows have you watched in the past three months?

6. You need to keep an eye out during your speech for audience _____.
   A. support   B. feedback
   C. appreciation   D. criticism

7. One of the ways speakers analyze the audience is by getting the traits such as age, gender, religion, group membership, and ethnic or cultural background. What is this kind of analysis called?
   A. Psychological audience analysis.
   B. Background audience analysis.
   C. Demographic audience analysis.
   D. Descriptive audience analysis.

8. Audience-centeredness involves keeping your audience foremost in mind _____.
   A. when you deliver your speech
   B. when you organize and outline your speech
   C. when you choose a topic for your speech
   D. at every step of speech preparation and presentation

9. The tendency of people to be concerned about all with their own values, beliefs, and well-being is called _____.
   A. ego-centrism
   B. ethnocentrism
   C. individualism
   D. plagiarism

10. _____ are the major factors in demographic audience analysis.
    A. Education, cultural background, interest in the topic, etc.,
    B. Physical setting, religion, and audience size
    C. Gender, age, education, economic standing, and cultural background
    D. Social status, ethnicity, and attitude toward the topic

2.3 Speaking Task: Making a Speech After Audience Analysis

Task I   Brainstorm a list of topics for an informative speech, and then choose one of the most appropriate topics to deliver a speech. Identify the kinds of information about the audience you need to make decisions about how you approach the speech.

Task II Suppose your school is going to invite Stephen E. Lucas, the editor-in-chief of *The Art of Public Speaking,* to give a lecture on the art of public speaking to college students from the English Department. You are required to write a speech of introduction to the guest speaker with about 300 words.

2.4 Self-Reflection: Audience Analysis and Adaptation

Evaluate your speech on audience analysis and adaptation. Rate your speech on each point: E—excellent, G—good, A—average, F—fair, P—poor.

Checklist: Audience Analysis and Adaptation

Items	Scores					Comments
	E	G	A	F	P	
Have you approached your speech from an audience-centered frame of mind?						
Have you considered all of the following in your audience analysis? (1) Size. (2) Physical setting and demographic traits. (3) Disposition toward you, toward the topic, and toward the occasion.						
If you have been invited to speak, have you learned about the history and mission of the group you will be addressing?						
If you are using an audience-analysis questionnaire, have you included the following question types? (1) Fixed-alternative questions. (2) Scale questions. (3) Open-ended questions.						
When preparing the speech, have you adapted to the audience so your ideas will be as clear and convincing as possible?						

Unit 3

Selecting a Topic and a Purpose

In this unit you will learn to:

- master the different methods of selecting appropriate speech topics;
- choose a worthwhile topic;
- write an effective general purpose and a specific purpose;
- formulate a strong central idea statement;
- write meaningful main points.

3.1 Speech Reading: Day of Infamy

Activity 1 Lead-in Listening

Listen to the speech and answer the following questions.

1. What is the hardest part of public speaking according to the speaker in the audio?

2. What are the factors a speaker should take into account when selecting a speech topic?

3. What is the most common skill you can use to come up with specific ideas for a speech topic?

Activity 2 Pre-reading Questions

1. How much do you know about Franklin D. Roosevelt?

2. Do you know anything about World War II?

3. What was the role of the United States in the Pacific Theater during World War II?

Day of Infamy[①][1]

1   Mr. Vice President, Mr. Speaker, and Members of the Senate and of the House of Representatives:

---

1 This text is adapted from Franklin D. Roosevelt's speech from the Thoughtco website.

2   Yesterday, December 7th, 1941—a date which will live in infamy—the United States of America was suddenly and **deliberately** attacked by **naval** and air forces of the Empire of Japan.

3   The United States was **at peace with** that nation and, at the **solicitation** of Japan, was still **in conversation with** its government and its emperor looking toward the maintenance of peace in the Pacific.

4   Indeed, one hour after Japanese air **squadrons** had **commenced** bombing in the American island of Oahu, the Japanese **ambassador** to the United States and his colleague delivered to our Secretary of State a formal reply to a recent American message. And while this reply stated that it seemed useless to continue the existing diplomatic negotiations, it contained no threat or hint of war or of armed attack.

5   It will be recorded that the distance of Hawaii from Japan makes it obvious that the attack was deliberately planned many days or even weeks ago. During the **intervening time**, the Japanese government has deliberately sought to deceive the United States by false statements and expressions of hope for continued peace.

6   The attack yesterday on the Hawaiian islands has caused severe damage to American naval and military forces. I regret to tell you that very many American lives have been lost. In addition, American ships have been reported **torpedoed** on the high seas between San Francisco and Honolulu.

7   Yesterday, the Japanese government also launched an attack against Malaya. Last night, Japanese forces attacked Hong Kong.

8   Last night, Japanese forces attacked Guam.

9   Last night, Japanese forces attacked the Philippine Islands.

10   Last night, the Japanese attacked Wake Island.

11   And this morning, the Japanese attacked Midway Island.

12   Japan has, therefore, undertaken a surprise offensive extending throughout the Pacific area. The facts of yesterday and today speak for themselves. The people of the United States have already formed their opinions and well understand the implications to the very life and safety of our nation.

13   As Commander in Chief of the Army and Navy, I have directed that all measures be taken for our defense. But always will our whole nation remember the character of the **onslaught** against us.

14   No matter how long it may take us to overcome this **premeditated** invasion, the American people in their righteous might will win through to absolute victory.

15   I believe that I interpret the will of the Congress and of the people when I assert that we will not only defend ourselves to the uttermost, but will make it very certain

that this form of **treachery** shall never again endanger us.

16 **Hostilities** exist. There is **no blinking at the fact that** our people, our territory, and our interests are **in grave danger**.

17 With confidence in our armed forces, with the unbounded determination of our people, we will gain the inevitable triumph—so help us God.

18 I ask that the Congress declare that since the unprovoked and **dastardly** attack by Japan on Sunday, December 7th, 1941, a state of war has existed between the United States and the Japanese empire.

> **Analysis**
>
> Ethos, pathos, and logos are all used extensively in the speech delivered by President Franklin D. Roosevelt on December 8th, 1941, which is called Day of Infamy.
>
> President Roosevelt establishes his credibility and authority as the Commander in Chief of the Army and Navy. His position in the government and his responsibility for national defense lend authority to his words. He also references the ongoing diplomatic negotiations, portraying the United States as a peaceful and reasonable nation that had been actively pursuing peaceful solutions with Japan. This reinforces his ethical appeal, emphasizing that the United States was not seeking conflict.
>
> Roosevelt turns to rich emotional appeal to achieve pathos. He evokes strong emotions by describing the attack on Pearl Harbor as "a date which will live in infamy" and emphasizing the loss of American lives and the severe damage to the naval and military forces. He paints a picture of the American people's determination and commitment to victory, appealing to the pride and unity of the nation. The phrase "so help us God" adds a solemn and emotional dimension to the speech, reinforcing the resolve of the American people.
>
> Roosevelt also uses logical appeals throughout the speech. He presents a chronological account of the events leading up to the attack and emphasizing the deliberate planning of the assault by Japan. By highlighting the deceptive actions of the Japanese government and their false statements, he builds a logical argument for why the United States must respond with force. His request to Congress to declare war is based on the rational conclusion that a state of war exists due to the unprovoked attack.
>
> In conclusion, the speech effectively employs ethos, pathos, and logos to convey the gravity of the situation and rally the American people to respond to the attack on Pearl Harbor. President Roosevelt establishes his credibility, appeals to emotions, and presents a logical argument for declaring war on Japan.

Unit 3　Selecting a Topic and a Purpose

Useful Words & Expressions

ambassador	n.	大使，使节
commence	v.	开始，着手
dastardly	adj.	卑鄙的，懦弱的
deliberately	adv.	故意地
hostility	n.	不友好
infamy	n.	声名狼藉，臭名昭著
naval	adj.	海军的
onslaught	n.	攻击
premeditate	v.	预谋，优先考虑
solicitation	n.	怂恿；请求
squadron	n.	中队（尤指空军）
torpedo	v.	用鱼雷攻击
treachery	n.	背叛，变节
at peace with sb.		与……和平共处
in conversation with		与……谈话
in grave danger		处于极大的危险之中
intervening time		两个事情之间的间隔时间
no blinking at the fact that...		毋庸讳言

Critical Thinking

1. How does selecting a topic influence the overall direction and effectiveness of a speech?

2. What is the significance of formulating a general and specific purpose statement for a speech? And how do they guide the speech's development?

3. In what ways does crafting a central idea or thesis statement help to unify and focus on a speech?

4. How can a speaker effectively draft main points that are supportive of the central idea and engaging for the audience?

5. How did the choice of topic in "Day of Infamy" reflect the American public's sentiments and values at that historical moment?

3.2 Skill Focus: Selecting a Topic and a Purpose

Before you get started to prepare your speech, you should first do the following: selecting a topic and a purpose, drafting a central idea, and drafting the main points.

3.2.1 Selecting a Topic

A speech topic is crucial to the success of the speech, which is determined by the occasion, the audience, and the qualifications of the speaker, so it is appropriate to choose the topics you know a lot, the topics you care about, or the topics the audience want to know.

The most common way that you choose a speech topic is to observe what is happening around. Generally, when selecting a topic, you can ask yourself some questions like "What do you know about?" and you can make a list of topics you have experience or knowledge about. Or you may ask yourself such questions as "What matters to you?" "What makes you excited or happy?" "What are you passionate about?", so that you can choose a speech topic from what you care about.

Bedsides, you can also ask yourself such questions as "What interests your audience?" "What matters to your audience right now?". This doesn't mean your audience has to be knowledgeable about your topic, but selecting a topic and tailoring it to their needs and interests will ensure an engaged audience.

If you still have some trouble picking a topic, the following ways can be used.

You can make a quick inventory of your experiences, interests, hobbies, skills, beliefs, and so on. Just take down whatever you can think of so that you are very likely to get a good topic from it.

Clustering sometimes works well in terms of topic selection. You just need to take out a piece of paper and divide it into nine columns: people, place, thing, event, process, concept, natural phenomenon, problem, and plan and policy.

Internet research is also a good way to select good themes like education, science, recreation, business, government, society, and culture, from which you can generate some good topics.

3.2.2 Selecting a Purpose

Once you have selected a topic, you should be very clear about your general purpose of making such a public speech. And once you have selected a general purpose, you must narrow down your topic to determine the specific purpose of your speech. The specific purpose should focus on one aspect of your topic, which can indicate precisely what you hope to accomplish through your speech.

1. General Purpose

The general purpose of the speech is often decided by the speaking situation, which can be divided into one of the four categories: to inform, to persuade, to entertain, and to commemorate or celebrate.

If your want to enhance the knowledge and understanding of the speech topic, the general purpose is to inform. Therefore, you should try to communicate information clearly, accurately, and interestingly to the audience and you are likely to work as a lecturer or a teacher.

If you want to change the audience's attitudes or actions towards something or some event, the general purpose is to persuade. Therefore, you should make every effort to win the audience over to your point of view and you probably work as an advocator or a partisan.

> **Example**
>
> Topic: The Newly Built Park
>
> General purpose 1: To inform.
>
> General purpose 2: To persuade.
>
> If you want to help the audience to understand the benefits the newly built park will bring to the citizens, the general purpose is to inform, but if you want to persuade your audience to make good use of the newly built park, the general purpose is to persuade.

2. Specific Purpose

A specific purpose indicates precisely what your speech seeks to achieve, which is based on your general purpose. So if your speech is an informative speech, the specific purpose is to inform your audience about a very specific realm of knowledge.

But how can you determine the specific purpose of a speech? Generally, you should take the main contributing elements into account and bring them together: interest, cultural background, experience and education, audience, context or setting, and so on. To write a specific purpose statement, you should follow the following principles: (1) be a full infinitive phrase; (2) be worded as a statement, not a question; (3) avoid figurative language; (4) never be vague or general; (5) be appropriate for your audience; (6) be achievable in the allotted time.

> **Example**
>
> Topic: The Newly Built Park
>
> General purpose 1: To inform.
>
> Specific purpose 1: To inform the audience of the benefits a newly built park will bring to the citizens.
>
> Suppose the city is going to build a new park for the citizens, and a lot of citizens oppose the proposal because they think that building a new park is only a total waste of time and money. When you deliver a speech, your first step is to inform the audience of the benefits a newly built park will bring to them.
>
> General purpose 2: To persuade.
>
> Specific purpose 2: To persuade the audience into making good use of the newly built park.
>
> Suppose the park has been built, but few citizens take advantage of the park. In this case, you can try to persuade the audience to make good use of the newly built park.

Writing a specific purpose statement is not always easy. Novice public speakers always have some problems in writing specific purpose statements, which can be listed as follows.

Problem 1: Some specific purpose statements try to cover too much and are too broad.

> **Example**
>
> Specific purpose: To inform your audience of Peking Opera.
>
> Problem: The specific purpose statement is too broad for a three-to-five-minute speech: it might be suitable for a three-hour lecture, or an entire course, but not for such a short presentation.
>
> Revised 1: To explain to your audience how Peking Opera came to be performed and studied in China.
>
> Revised 2: To explain to your audience how Peking Opera originated as an art form in China.
>
> The revised specific purpose statements are much more manageable when you are given the limited amount of time.

Unit 3 Selecting a Topic and a Purpose

Problem 2: Some specific purpose statements are too narrow that they might only be appropriate for people who are already extremely interested in the topic or those who are experts in a field.

> **Example**
>
> Specific purpose: To inform your audience of the life cycle of a new species of lima bean.
> Problem: The specific statement is so focused that it is only appropriate for botanists or agriculturalists who have an interest in it.
> Revised: To inform your audience of the life cycle of a dog.

Problem 3: The "communication verb" in the specific purpose does not match the content.

> **Example 1**
>
> Specific purpose: To inform your audience why capital punishment is unconstitutional.
> Problem: This cannot be informative since it is taking a side.
> Revised: To persuade your audience that capital punishment should be unconstitutional.
>
> **Example 2**
>
> Specific purpose: To persuade your audience about the three types of individual retirement accounts.
> Problem: This is not persuading, but informing the audience of the three types of individual retirement accounts.
> Revised: To inform your audience of the three types of individual retirement accounts.
>
>   The two examples mentioned above show that the persuasive content is paired with "to inform" or "to explain" and the informative content is paired with "to persuade".

Problem 4: The specific purpose statement has two parts, or it covers two different topics.

> **Example**
>
> Specific purpose: To explain to your audience how to swing a golf club and choose the best golf shoes.
> Problem: The specific purpose statement covers two different topics.
> Revised: To explain to your audience how to swing a golf club.
>   To explain to your audience how to choose the best golf shoes.

A well-crafted specific purpose statement is essential for delivering an effective speech, as it serves as a guide for writing and acts as an outline to keep you on track during the delivery. It helps to prevent you from straying off the topic and ensures that your message remains focused.

It is important to distinguish the general purpose and the specific purpose of a speech. While the general purpose statement outlines the broader goal of the speech, the specific purpose statement provides a precise description of what the speech aims to achieve. Both types of purposes are crucial in preparing a speech.

3.2.3 Drafting a Central Idea

When preparing a speech, you should clearly articulate your focus and main points based on the specific purpose of your speech. This can be achieved through the use of the central idea statement, which is commonly known as the central idea. A central idea statement is a simple, declarative sentence that refines and clarifies the specific purpose statement. It encapsulates the main points of your speech and usually emerges after the thorough research and decision-making regarding your key messages. In most cases, a central idea statement succinctly summarizes all the main points in a single declarative sentence.

Crafting a clear central idea is crucial to capture the attention of your audience and encourage them to engage with your topic. To create an effective central idea, you should consider the following into consideration: (1) ensure that the central idea is not too vague or ambiguous; (2) express the central idea as a complete sentence; (3) use a declarative sentence structure instead of a question; (4) avoid using figurative language in the central idea.

> **Example 1**
>
> General purpose: To inform.
> Specific purpose: To inform the benefits of pet ownership for mental health and well-being.
> Central idea: Owning a pet can have numerous positive effects on an individual's mental health and overall well-being, including reducing stress, anxiety, and depression, as well as increasing the feelings of happiness, and social connectedness.
>
> **Example 2**
>
> General purpose: To persuade.

> Specific purpose: To persuade developers, and policymakers as a whole to carefully consider and address the ethical implications of AI technology in order to ensure that its benefits are maximized and its potential risks are minimized.
>
> Central idea: The development and deployment of AI technology carry significant ethical implications and require the involvement and cooperation of developers, and policymakers as a whole in order to establish ethical guidelines, regulations, and best practices for AI development and use.
>
> From the above examples, you can see a central idea is much more specific than the general purpose and the specific purpose. It can catch the attention of the audience and engage them in thinking about your topic.

3.2.4 Drafting the Main Points

After you finish drafting the central idea, you should make an outline of your speech, planning what you want to say in each paragraph and what evidence you will use. Then you can draft a topic sentence that sums up the main point of each paragraph, and then the rest of the paragraph should flow logically from the main point, expanding on the point with evidence, examples, or statistics.

A topic sentence gives the main idea of a paragraph, which is usually at the beginning of a paragraph. A good topic sentence is specific enough to give a clear sense of what to expect from the paragraph. Generally, a topic sentence has the following characteristics such as being clearly independent of each other, using the same pattern of wording for the topic sentence, and limiting the number of main points from two to five. A topic sentence should include two key things: the topic of the paragraph and the main point of the paragraph.

> **Example**
>
> Suppose you are writing a five-paragraph speech script about "The Environmental Impacts of Dietary Choices". Here are three topic sentences which can be used for each of the three body paragraphs.
>
> Topic: The Environmental Impacts of Dietary Choices
>
> Central idea: Food is an increasingly urgent environmental issue, and to reduce human's impact on the planet, it is necessary to change global patterns of food production and consumption.

> Topic sentences:
>
> (1) Research has shown that the meat industry has severe environmental impacts.
>
> (2) However, many plant-based foods are also produced in environmentally damaging ways.
>
> (3) It's important to consider not only what type of diet you eat, but where your food comes from and how it is produced.

The following are some tips on how to write good main points of a speech.

(1) Make sure the main point isn't too vague.

> **Example**
>
> Main point 1: In *Pride and Prejudice*, Mr. Bingley seems like a nice guy.
>
> Main point 2: When Mr. Bingley is first introduced, he comes across as a kind person because he speaks to everyone and doesn't immediately pass judgment.

(2) Choose a reasonable opinion.

> **Example**
>
> Main point 1: It's obvious that Mr. Bingley was a total loser with no backbone.
>
> Main point 2: Mr. Bingley could have shown more confidence in his choices and stood up to Mr. Darcy when he found himself in love with Jane Bennet.

(3) Use transition words in your main point to show the connections between your ideas.

> **Example**
>
> Main point 1: Mr. Bingley is a good man and here's why.
>
> Main point 2: Although Mr. Bingley did break Jane's heart by leaving, he ended up redeeming himself by returning to Netherfield Hall.

The following is an example on how you can develop the topic sentence, the general purpose, the specific purpose, the central idea and the main points step by step.

Unit 3 Selecting a Topic and a Purpose

> **Example**
>
> Topic: Swimming
>
> General purpose: To persuade.
>
> Specific purpose: To persuade the audience to go swimming.
>
> Central idea: You should go swimming as much as possible because swimming can help you to improve your heart health, reduce your stress and anxiety, and maintain your healthy weight.
>
> Main Points:
>
> (1) Swimming is a low-impact exercise that can help you to improve heart health and reduce the risk of heart disease by strengthening the heart and improving blood circulation.
>
> (2) Swimming can be a relaxing and meditative activity that can help to reduce stress and anxiety.
>
> (3) Swimming is an excellent way to burn calories and lose weight or maintain a healthy weight.

After you formulate an effective central idea and write the main points, you are on the track to give a satisfactory public speech to the audience.

Exercises

I. Decide whether the following statements are TRUE (T), FALSE (F) or NOT GIVEN (NG) according to the Skill Focus in this unit.

1. A speech of introduction for the guest speaker should provide his or her background, personality, beliefs, goals, etc. (   )

2. The introduction of a speech is good enough so long as it can gain the audience's attention and interest of the topic you are going to deliver. (   )

3. An introductory speech can be organized either in chronological order or topical order. (   )

4. The central idea of a speech is usually formulated before the specific purpose. (   )

5. After choosing a topic, the next step in speech preparation is determining your specific purpose. (   )

6. The central idea of a speech should be expressed using a full sentence. (   )

7. The specific purpose statement indicates precisely what you hope to accomplish in a speech. (   )

8. The specific purpose reveals more about the content of a speech than the central idea does. (   )

9. "To inform your audience about depression" is an example of an effective specific purpose statement for a speech. (   )

10. The difference between informing and persuading is like the difference between teaching and advocating. (   )

II. Choose the best options to answer the following question or fill in the blanks according to the information given in this unit.

1. When you have trouble in selecting a topic, which of the following is the effective method of generating ideas for speech topics?
   A. Clustering.　　　　　　　　　B. A personal inventory.
   C. An Internet search.　　　　　　D. All of the above.

2. _____ is a way of generating ideas for speech topics by free association of words and ideas.
   A. Imaging　　　　　　　　　　B. Brainstorming
   C. Channeling　　　　　　　　　D. Clustering

3. When you work as a teacher or lecturer, your general purpose is to _____ for a class.
   A. inform　　　　　　　　　　　B. persuade
   C. entertain　　　　　　　　　　D. commemorate

4. When you want to change your friend's attitude towards public speaking, your general purpose is to _____.
   A. inform　　　　　　　　　　　B. persuade
   C. entertain　　　　　　　　　　D. commemorate

5. The _____ is a single infinitive phrase that states precisely what a speaker hopes to accomplish in his or her speech.
   A. general purpose statement　　　B. specific purpose statement
   C. central idea　　　　　　　　　D. introductory statement

6. The _____ is a one-sentence statement that sums up or encapsulates the main point of a speech.
   A. central idea　　　　　　　　　B. general purpose statement
   C. internal summary　　　　　　　D. specific purpose statement

7. When you act as an advocate or a partisan, your general purpose is to _____.
   A. inform
   B. persuade
   C. entertain
   D. commemorate

8. Speeches that you deliver will be either to inform, to persuade, or to entertain. This goal for your speech is known as its _____.
   A. general purpose
   B. specific purpose
   C. central idea
   D. blueprint

9. In Barnett's speech outline appeared the sentence: "Censorship of the music industry violates our First Amendment right to free speech.", it can be recognized as _____.
   A. a general purpose statement
   B. a specific purpose statement
   C. a central idea or thesis
   D. an inflammatory statement

10. The first step of the introduction is _____.
    A. to reveal the topic
    B. a preview of the main idea
    C. to get the audience's attention
    D. to establish credibility

3.3 Speaking Task: Make a Speech Developed from a Topic

Task Brainstorm a list of informative or persuasive speech topics. Choose one topic and develop a speech composition from the general purpose, the specific purpose, the central idea, the main points, and finally the speech composition step by step.

The following are some steps for your reference.

To start with, brainstorm a list of topics which are interesting and informative for your audience to learn about. Some examples can be climate change, mental health, social justice, technology, or personal growth. When you have a list of potential topics, choose one that you are passionate about and feel confident in.

Next, consider the specific purpose of your speech. Are you trying to inform your audience about a particular issue or persuade them to take action on a certain topic? Be clear about your goal so that you can tailor your message accordingly.

Then, develop a central idea for your speech that encapsulates the main point you want to convey. This should be a clear and concise statement that summarizes the purpose of your speech and what you hope your audience will take away from it. Identify the main points you want to cover in your speech. These should be specific examples or arguments that support your central idea and help to illustrate your message. Make sure each main point is relevant to your audience and supports your overall purpose.

Finally, begin drafting your speech by organizing your main points into a logical order. Start with an attention-grabbing opening that hooks your audience and sets the tone for the rest of your speech. Introduce your central idea and main points in a clear and concise manner. Use evidence, statistics, or personal anecdotes to support your arguments and engage your audience. End with a strong closing that reinforces your central idea and encourages your audience to take action or think differently about the topic.

3.4 Self-Reflection: Evaluating the Specific Purpose and the Central Idea Statements

Evaluate the specific purpose of your speech based on the following rubrics.

Items	Yes	No
Is the specific purpose written as a full infinitive phrase?		
Is the specific purpose phrased as a statement rather than a question?		
Is the specific purpose free from the figurative language?		
Does the specific purpose indicate precisely what you plan to accomplish in the speech?		
Is the specific purpose suitable for your audience?		
Can the specific purpose be accomplished in the time allotted for the speech?		

Evaluate the central idea of your speech based on the following rubrics.

Items	Yes	No
Is the central idea written as a complete sentence?		
Is the central idea phrased as a statement rather than a question?		
Is the central idea free from the figurative language?		
Does the central idea clearly encapsulate the main points to be discussed in the body of the speech?		
Is the central idea suitable for your audience?		
Can the central idea be adequately discussed in the time allotted for the speech?		

Unit 4

Organizing a Speech

In this unit you will learn to:

- differentiate various organizational patterns (chronological, topical, spatial, and causal patterns);
- highlight the importance of aligning pattern choice with the specific purpose of the speech;
- provide examples of when certain patterns are more suitable than others;
- emphasize how a logical pattern enhances the overall coherence and impact of a speech.

4.1 Speech Reading: Stay Hungry, Stay Foolish

Activity 1 Lead-in Listening

Listen to the speech and write down its mind map.

Activity 2 Pre-reading Questions

1. What is the primary purpose of college education when individuals prepare for their future careers and personal development?

2. How does college education contribute to the acquisition of specialized knowledge and skills within specific fields of study?

3. In what ways does college education foster problem-solving abilities?

Stay Hungry, Stay Foolish[1]

1 The first story is about connecting the dots.

2 I **dropped out** of Reed College① after the first 6 months, but then stayed around as a drop-in for another 18 months or so before I really quit. So why did I drop out?

---

1 This text is adapted from the Bilibili website.

3   It started before I was born. My **biological** mother was a young, **unwed** college graduate student, and she decided to put me up for adoption. She felt very strongly that I should be adopted by college graduates, so everything was all set for me to be adopted at birth by a lawyer and his wife. Except that when I popped out they decided at the last minute that they really wanted a girl.

4   So my parents, who were on a waiting list, got a call in the middle of the night asking: "We have an unexpected baby boy; do you want him?" They said: "Of course." My biological mother later found out that my mother had never graduated from college and that my father had never graduated from high school. She refused to sign the final adoption papers. She only relented a few months later when my parents promised that I would go to college. This was a start in my life.

5   And 17 years later I did go to college. But I naively chose a college that was almost as expensive as Stanford, and all of my working-class parents' savings were being spent on my college tuition. After six months, I couldn't see the value in it. I had no idea what I wanted to do with my life and no idea how college was going to help me figure it out.

6   And here I was spending all of the money my parents had saved during their entire life. So I decided to drop out and trust that it would all work out OK. It was pretty scary at the time, but looking back it was one of the best decisions I ever made. The minute I dropped out I could stop taking the required classes that didn't interest me, and begin dropping in on the ones that looked far more interesting.

7   It wasn't all romantic. I didn't have a dorm room, so I slept on the floor in friends' rooms, I returned coke bottles for the 5 cent deposits to buy food with, and I would walk the 7 miles across town every Sunday night to get one good meal a week at the Hare Krishna temple. I loved it. And much of what I stumbled into by following my curiosity and intuition turned out to be priceless later on. Let me give you one example:

8   Reed College at that time offered perhaps the best **calligraphy** instruction in the country. Throughout the campus, every poster and every label on every drawer were beautifully designed. Because I had dropped out and didn't have to take the normal classes, I decided to take a calligraphy class to learn how to do this.

9   I learned about Serif and Sans Serif[2] typefaces, about varying the amount of space between different letter combinations, about what makes great **typography** great. It was beautiful, historical, artistically subtle in a way that science can't capture, and I found it fascinating.

10 None of this had even a hope of any practical application in my life. But ten years later, when we were designing the first Macintosh computer, it all came back

to me. And we designed it all into the Mac. It was the first computer with beautiful typography. If I had never dropped in on that single course in college, the Mac would have never had multiple typefaces or **proportionally** spaced fonts.

11 And since Windows just copied the Mac, it's likely that no personal computer would have them. If I had never dropped out, I would have never dropped in on this calligraphy class, and personal computers might not have the wonderful typography that they do. Of course it was impossible to connect the dots looking forward when I was in college. But it was very, very clear looking backwards ten years later.

12 Again, you can't connect the dots looking forward; you can only connect them looking backwards. So you have to trust that the dots will somehow connect in your future. You have to trust in something—your gut, destiny, life, karma, and whatever. This approach has never let me down, and it has made all the difference in my life.

Analysis

The speech is delivered by Steve Jobs where he reflects on his life and the choices he made. He talks about dropping out of Reed College and how he didn't see the value in college at that time. He describes his experiences after dropping out, including sleeping on friends' room floors, learning calligraphy, and so on. He emphasizes that he followed his curiosity and intuition, even though he couldn't see the practical applications of his interests at that time. He gives an example of how his calligraphy knowledge from college influenced the design of the Macintosh computer's typography, which had a significant impact on the personal computer industry. He concludes by encouraging the audience to trust that the dots will connect in the future, even if they can't see it at the moment.

The argument in the article is effective due to its use of supporting evidences and personal anecdotes. Steve Jobs used his own experiences to illustrate his points, making the argument relatable and engaging. The example of how his calligraphy class later influenced the design of the Macintosh computer serves as a strong evidence for his message. This concrete and specific example shows how seemingly unrelated experiences can come together in unexpected ways to shape future outcomes. By sharing his personal journey and the pivotal moments that led to his success, Jobs provides a clear and persuasive argument for the idea that one's experiences and choices can have a meaningful impact on his future, even if the connections are not immediately apparent.

Additionally, the argument benefits from Jobs' use of rhetorical devices, such as repetition and appeals to emotion. These elements help to create a compelling narrative and drive home the central message of the speech. The article effectively combines personal anecdotes, concrete examples, and rhetorical techniques together to deliver a persuasive speech about the importance of trusting one's intuition and experiences in shaping his or her own future.

Useful Words & Expression

biological	adj.	亲生的
calligraph	v.	以书法书写或印刷
proportionally	adv.	与……成比例地
typography	n.	排印；版式
unwed	adj.	未婚的
drop out		停止，中断；退出

Notes

① Reed College: It was founded in 1908 and is a private, independent liberal arts college located in the southeastern part of Portland, Oregon, United States.

② Serif and Sans Serif: In Western countries where the Roman alphabet is used, typefaces are divided into two major categories: Serif and Sans Serif. Although typewriters also belong to the Sans Serif category, they are distinct due to being Monospace fonts, hence the separate category of Monospace. Serif refers to the additional decorations at the beginning and end of the strokes of the letters, and the thickness of the strokes varies depending on whether they are vertical or horizontal. In contrast, Sans Serif lacks these extra decorations, with strokes having a more uniform thickness.

Critical Thinking

1. How does the organization of a speech affect the audience's emotional and intellectual engagement with the topic?

2. What are the key factors to consider when choosing an organizational structure for a speech? How do these factors vary depending on the audience and the speech's objectives?

3. How can the principles of effective speech organization make sense in the speech delivery?

4. What are the potential challenges in organizing a speech that addresses controversial or complex topics? How can these challenges be overcome?

5. In the context of "Stay Hungry, Stay Foolish", how does the effective organization of Steve Jobs' speech contribute to his ability to persuade and influence the audience?

4.2 Skill Focus: Organizing a Speech

As you progress in crafting a speech, it is the turn to contemplate the organization of your speech. The manner in which you organize your speech holds profound significance, determining the clarity and coherence of the message you intend to convey. By meticulously organizing your speech, you pave the way for the audience experience that is both comprehensible and engaging.

Considering various methods of organization is vital as it serves as a roadmap for your ideas. It empowers you to arrange concepts in a logical sequence, allowing the audience to grasp your thoughts easily. Moreover, a well-structured speech exudes professionalism and competence. It reflects the respect you hold for your audience's time and attention. By adhering to a coherent framework, you make the journey through your discourse smooth and intuitive.

4.2.1 Chronological Pattern

The chronological pattern, often referred to as the temporal pattern, offers a logical and intuitive way to structure your content while harnessing the power of chronological sequencing.

Chronological pattern involves presenting your main points in the order they occurred, and aligning them with the passage of time as if they were plotted on a calendar or clock. This pattern is particularly beneficial when conveying historical narratives or events that follow a temporal sequence. Whether you're narrating a historical account or outlining the steps of a process, the chronological pattern proves invaluable in facilitating comprehension.

By adopting a chronological pattern, you enable your audience to traverse time alongside your narrative, vividly visualizing the progression of events and their significance when you deliver a speech about historical events. The logical ordering aids understanding and helps the audience to contextualize each event within the broader historical context. Furthermore, this pattern finds its niche in informative speeches where the subject matter necessitates a step-by-step approach. Think of informative speeches that walk the audience through a series of events or processes—the chronological style is a natural fit.

The chronological pattern can also be applied to process speeches, where a clear and sequential presentation of steps is crucial for audience comprehension. It can ensure a coherent arrangement of each stage, facilitating a seamless understanding of the overall process's evolution. Similarly, the chronological pattern is equally suitable for narrating an individual's life journey, which not only illuminates his or her critical life events but also emphasizes the inherent progression.

In essence, the chronological pattern is a powerful ally in your public speaking arsenal. It caters to narratives that hinge on time-bound sequences, ensuring that your audience embarks on a cohesive journey through events, processes, or life stories. By using this pattern, you not only enhance comprehension but also immerse your audience in the unfolding narrative, making your speech a memorable and impactful experience.

Example

Specific Purpose: To inform the audience about the development of artificial intelligence (AI) chronologically.

(1) The Birth of AI (1950s–1960s): The concept of AI was born in the mid-20th century, with the Dartmouth Conference in 1956 being a pivotal moment. Early AI research focused on problem-solving and symbolic methods, with the development of the first AI program, the Logic Theorist, by Allen Newell and Herbert Simon.

(2) Early AI Boom and Expert Systems (1970s–1980s): This period was characterized by the rise of "expert systems", which mimicked the decision-making abilities of a human expert in a specific domain. These systems used rule-based logic and were successful in various industries, leading to optimism about AI's potential.

(3) AI Winter (late 1980s–1990s): Despite initial enthusiasm, the limitations of rule-based systems became apparent, and progress slowed due to the complexity of real-world problems. Funding for AI research decreased, marking a period known as the "AI Winter".

(4) Machine Learning Renaissance (late 1990s–2000s): With the advent of machine learning, AI research was revitalized. Algorithms like neural networks began to show promise in handling complex data and patterns. The development of support vector machines and other statistical methods marked a shift towards data-driven AI.

(5) Big Data and Deep Learning (2010s): The availability of vast amounts of data, coupled with increased computational power, led to the rise of deep learning. Neural networks with many layers, known as deep neural networks, became capable of learning from and making decisions based on large datasets, revolutionizing fields like computer vision and natural language processing.

(6) AI Integration and Automation (2010s–present): AI has become increasingly

> integrated into everyday life, from virtual assistants to recommendation systems. Automation in various sectors, including manufacturing, healthcare, and finance, is being driven by AI advancements.

4.2.2 Spatial Pattern

Compared with the chronological pattern, which is grounded in your innate grasp of time's progression and sequence, the spatial pattern stems from your aptitude to comprehend movement and direction within the physical realm. Both the chronological and spatial patterns tap into your innate cognitive processes that shape your understanding. The chronological pattern smoothly organizes events over time, while the spatial pattern facilitates mental navigation through the physical world. These patterns are not mutually exclusive; they can harmoniously intertwine to create narratives with greater depth. This harmonious fusion resonates with the audience, offering multi-dimensional comprehension aligned with your cognitive foundations.

> **Example**
>
> Specific purpose: To explain to your classmates the three economic zones.
>
> (1) The Eastern Economic Zone is home to developed cities such as Shanghai and Beijing, which are major financial and commercial centers.
>
> (2) The Central Economic Zone is known for its manufacturing industries, including electronics and machinery.
>
> (3) The Western Economic Zone encompasses a vast agricultural area and is considered the heartland of China's economy.

Unlike the temporal orientation, your cognitive abilities extend to interpret movement and direction in physical space. The spatial pattern leverages this capacity to present information based on the tangible relationships between objects and concepts. This pattern finds its niche in descriptions, instructions, and narratives that hinge on location and arrangement.

As for public speaking, selecting the appropriate organizational pattern resembles choosing a lens through which your message is perceived. Whether conveying a historical account, guiding your audience through a physical space, or merging elements of time and space, the chosen pattern molds the narrative's clarity and impact. It's akin to offering your audience a cognitive roadmap that leads them through your content with clarity and resonance.

The human mind's inclination towards time-orientation and spatial perception has birthed the effective organizational constructs of the chronological and spatial patterns. These patterns serve as cognitive bridges, uniting your message with the audience's comprehension. By harnessing these patterns, communication transcends mere transmission; it aligns with the innate cognitive processes, crafting narratives that will resonate, captivate, and endure in the minds of the audience.

4.2.3 Topical Pattern

Speeches are a powerful medium of communication, used to convey information, persuade, entertain, or inspire. Effective organization is the backbone of a compelling speech, and one versatile approach is the topical organizational pattern. This pattern is probably the most all-purpose, as it can be applied to a wide range of speech topics. It allows speakers to divide their main points into categories, types, kinds, or sorts, providing clarity and structure to their message.

The topical organizational pattern is a flexible structure that can accommodate a multitude of subjects and speech purposes. Whether you're giving a speech on the diversity of animal species, the history of music genres, or the benefits of exercise, the topical pattern can be of great help. It provides a clear roadmap for both you and the audience, making it easier to understand, follow, and remember the key points. When the topical pattern is used in a speech, it is important to maintain simplicity, clarity, and distinctiveness.

One of the primary strengths of the topical pattern is its ability to categorize information effectively. Many subjects can be divided into various types, kinds, sorts, or categories, making it easier for the audience to digest complex content.

Examples

(1) The world of flora and fauna can be categorized into different types of ecosystems, species of animals, or families of plants.

(2) Music genres can be sorted into categories like classical, jazz, rock, pop, and hip-hop.

(3) In a speech about healthy eating, you might explore different kinds of diets, such as vegetarian, Mediterranean, or Keto.

(4) A discussion about renewable energy sources can be organized into categories like solar, wind, hydro, and geothermal power.

(5) Specific purpose: To explain to your freshmen students the concept of SMART goals.
SMART goals are specific.

> SMART goals are measurable.
>
> SMART goals are achievable.
>
> SMART goals are relevant.
>
> SMART goals are time-bound.

4.2.4 Causal Pattern and Effect Pattern

Causal pattern and effect pattern are also two useful ones that can be used in the speech delivery. Understanding when to use them is essential to convey your message effectively. When crafting a speech with a causal pattern, your primary focus is on uncovering the causes, origins, roots, foundations, basis, grounds, or sources of a particular phenomenon. This pattern aims to answer the question: "Why does this happen?". Let's dive deeper into the key points of a causal pattern.

1. Casual Pattern

1) Identifying Causes

The central objective of a speech organized in a causal pattern is to identify the causes behind a specific event, situation, or outcome. It delves into the causes that lead to the observed result.

> **Example**
>
> Suppose you're delivering a speech about the causes of climate change. In this speech, you can explore factors like greenhouse gas emissions, deforestation, and industrial pollution as the underlying causes of the phenomenon.

2) Explaining Origins

Speeches using causal pattern often involve a historical or chronological exploration of the origins of a particular issue. This provides the audience with a contextual understanding of how and when it all began.

> **Example**
>
> If your speech topic is the origins of the Internet, you can take your audience on a journey through the early days of computer networking to the development of the World Wide Web.

3) Analyzing Foundations

To create a comprehensive causal pattern speech, you need to analyze the foundations upon which an event or phenomenon is built. This involves examining the fundamental principles or concepts that underpin the subject matter.

> **Example**
>
> When discussing the foundations of the value education, you've explored the philosophy of education, ethical and moral frameworks, cultural and societal values, character education, and integration into the curriculum and pedagogy.

In contrast to causal pattern, effect pattern in speech organization focuses on uncovering the effects, results, outcomes, consequences, or products of a particular phenomenon. The primary question addressed in effect pattern is: "What happens as a result?". Let's explore the key points of an effect pattern.

2. Effect Pattern

1) Revealing Consequences

Speeches organized in an effect pattern emphasize the consequences or outcomes of a specific event, action, or decision. They aim to highlight the results that follow from certain circumstances.

> **Example**
>
> If your speech is about the consequences of deforestation, you can discuss the impact on biodiversity loss, climate change, and habitat destruction.

2) Exploring Outcomes

Effect pattern speeches often involve an exploration of the various outcomes that arise from a particular situation. This includes both intended and unintended consequences.

> **Example**
>
> When discussing the outcomes of a well-executed marketing campaign, you can highlight increased brand recognition, higher sales, and enhanced customer loyalty.

3) Analyzing Products

To create an informative effect pattern speech, it's essential to analyze the products or tangible results generated by a process or action. This provides the audience with a clear understanding of the practical implications.

> **Example**
>
> If your speech focuses on the products of scientific research, you can discuss innovations, technologies, and discoveries that have emerged as a result of scientific inquiry.

In some cases, a speech may require an exploration of both the causes and effects of a particular phenomenon. This cause and effect pattern seeks to provide a comprehensive view of the subject matter, addressing both "why" and "what happens as a result". The following should be taken into consideration when delivering a cause-and-effect pattern speech.

1) Balancing Causes and Effects

When crafting a cause-and-effect pattern speech, it's essential to strike a balance between the factors that lead to a particular outcome and the consequences that result from the factors.

> **Example**
>
> If you're delivering a speech about the cause and effect of global economic recessions, you can first discuss factors like financial speculation and unsustainable debt (causes) and then delve into the economic downturn, unemployment, and market crashes (effects).

2) Providing Contextual Understanding

A cause and effect pattern speech offers the audience a holistic understanding of a complex issue by presenting both the contextual background and the resulting impact.

> **Example**
>
> In the speech about the cause and effect of the Industrial Revolution, you can first explain the societal changes and innovations that sparked the Industrial Revolution (causes) and then explore the consequences, such as urbanization and changes in labor practices (effects).

3. Tips for Making an Informed Decision

Choosing between causal pattern, effect pattern, or a combination of both depends on your specific purpose and the nature of your speech topic. Here are some tips to help you to make an informed decision.

1) Analyzing Your Specific Purpose

Before delivering a speech, you should examine your specific purpose first. If your goal is to explain why something occurs, a causal pattern may be appropriate. If you aim to discuss the results or outcomes of a particular situation, effect pattern is more suitable.

2) Understanding Your Audience

Consider the needs and expectations of your audience. What information are they seeking? Are they more interested in understanding the reasons behind a phenomenon or the consequences? Tailor your organizational pattern to meet their interests.

3) Evaluating the Complexity of the Topic

Complex topics may benefit from a cause and effect pattern, as it provides a comprehensive view of the subject matter. Simpler topics may require a more straightforward approach, either focusing on causes or focusing on effects.

4) Maintaining Clarity and Coherence

Regardless of the organizational pattern you choose, it's essential to maintain clarity and coherence throughout your speech. Clearly signal transitions between causes and effects to guide your audience seamlessly through your presentation.

In summary, the utilization of organizational patterns is akin to building a sturdy framework that lends shape and coherence to your speech. These patterns aren't merely arbitrary guidelines, but they are strategic tools that enable you to orchestrate your thoughts and speech content in a manner that resonates with your audience's understanding.

As you embark on crafting impactful speeches, remember that the choice of organizational pattern isn't just a technical detail, but it's a strategic decision that can elevate the resonance of your message. The harmonious synergy between content and structure transforms your speech from a mere presentation into an immersive experience, bridging the gap between you and the audience.

Exercises

Choose the best options to answer the following questions or fill in the blanks according to the information given in this unit.

1. What is the primary focus of the text?
   A. Discussing the importance of public speaking.
   B. Analyzing cognitive processes in communication.

C. Exploring the role of spatial patterns in speeches.

　　D. Examining the organizational patterns in speeches.

2. Why is organizing speech material important?

　　A. It impresses the audience with complexity.

　　B. It adds a creative touch to the speech.

　　C. It enhances the clarity and coherence of the message.

　　D. It makes the speech longer and more detailed.

3. Which of the following is NOT mentioned as a benefit of a well-structured speech?

　　A. It aids retention.

　　B. It fosters engagement.

　　C. It helps you to save time.

　　D. It empowers effective communication.

4. What does the chronological organization pattern primarily focus on?

　　A. Relationships between objects and concepts.

　　B. Sequences of events based on time.

　　C. Spatial perception.

　　D. Cognitive processes.

5. When might the spatial pattern be particularly useful in a speech?

　　A. When discussing a historical narrative.

　　B. When explaining a step-by-step process.

　　C. When presenting a problem and its solutions.

　　D. When discussing abstract concept.

6. How can the chronological and spatial patterns be used together in a speech?

　　A. To confuse the audience with conflicting information.

　　B. To create narratives with greater depth.

　　C. To increase the length of the speech.

　　D. To make the speech more complex.

7. What is the purpose of selecting an organizational pattern in public speaking?

　　A. To confuse the audience.

　　B. To offer the audience a cognitive roadmap.

　　C. To limit the audience's comprehension.

　　D. To make the speech longer.

8. Which of the following statements is TRUE about the spatial pattern in speeches?

　　A. It primarily focuses on sequences of events.

　　B. It immerses the audience in the unfolding narrative.

　　C. It is not aligned with your cognitive foundations.

D. It is exclusive to informative speeches.

9. What is the analogy used to describe the selection of the organizational pattern in public speaking?
   A. Choosing a musical instrument.
   B. Selecting a cognitive lens.
   C. Picking a random direction.
   D. Deciding on a random topic.

10. What is the fundamental purpose of the organizational pattern in speeches?
    A. To complicate the message.
    B. To confuse the audience.
    C. To align with cognitive processes and enhance clarity.
    D. To entertain the audience.

11. Why do people tend to organize information chronologically and spatially?
    A. Because of cultural influence.
    B. Because of biological basis
    C. Because of human mind's inclination.
    D. Because of cognitive simplicity.

12. What is the topical organizational pattern primarily used for?
    A. Uncovering causes and origins.
    B. Dividing main points into categories.
    C. Explaining the consequences of events.
    D. Emphasizing chronological sequencing.

13. How many categories should be maintained when using the topical pattern?
    A. As many as possible for comprehensive coverage.
    B. At least seven to provide depth.
    C. Five or fewer to ensure simplicity and clarity.
    D. Ten or more for variety.

14. What is the primary strength of the topical pattern?
    A. Its ability to uncover causes and origins.
    B. Its flexibility in accommodating various subjects.
    C. Its emphasis on chronological sequencing.
    D. Its focus on the consequences of events.

15. What is the main focus of a speech organized with a causal pattern?
    A. Identifying causes and origins.
    B. Explaining the consequences of events.
    C. Analyzing the products of a process.

D. Describing chronological sequences.

16. Which organizational pattern is suitable when discussing the results or outcomes of a particular situation?
    A. Causal pattern.   B. Effect pattern.
    C. Topical pattern.   D. Chronological pattern.

17. What does a cause-and-effect pattern speech seek to address?
    A. The consequences of events only.
    B. The origins of specific phenomena only.
    C. Both the reasons behind events and their consequences.
    D. A chronological sequence of events.

18. How does the article suggest choosing an organizational pattern for a speech?
    A. By selecting the most complex pattern available.
    B. By considering the chronological sequence of events.
    C. By aligning it with your specific purpose and audience needs.
    D. By using visual aids to guide the audience.

19. What is the primary purpose of the organizational patterns in speeches?
    A. To complicate the speech content.
    B. To serve as arbitrary guidelines.
    C. To create confusion among the audience.
    D. To lend shape and coherence to the speech.

20. According to the article, what does the choice of organizational pattern in a speech reflect?
    A. Your creativity.
    B. Your desire for complexity.
    C. The thoughtfulness invested in catering to the audience's cognitive journey.
    D. Your preference for chronological sequencing.

4.3　Speaking Task: Making a Speech About Ren in Confucianism

Task　Some people say that in our modern and fast-paced society, the traditional concept of Ren, or benevolence, is no longer relevant. To what extent do you agree or disagree? Deliver a speech to illustrate your opinion.

4.4 Self-Reflection: Evaluating the Organization of Your Speech

Evaluate your speech based on how well you meet each specific criterion. Rate your speech on each point: E—excellent, G—good, A—average, F—fair, P—poor.

Checklist: Organization of Your Speech

Items	Scores					Comments
	E	G	A	F	P	
Introduction						
Gaining attention						
Introducing the topic clearly						
Relating the topic to the audience						
Establishing credibility						
Body						
Main points with clarity						
Main points support materials						
Organization planning						
Clear and appropriate language						
Effective connectives						
Transitions between main points						
Use of examples and evidence						
Conclusion						
Preparing audience for ending						
Summarizing main points						
Reinforcing central idea						
Calling to action or closing statement						
Delivery						
Strong eye contact						
Engaged facial expressions						
Gestures and body language						

(To be continued)

(Continued)

Items	Scores					Comments
	E	G	A	F	P	
Clear articulation						
Varied vocal tone and pace						
Effective use of pauses						
Controlled nervousness						
Overall confidence and presence						

Unit 5

Opening and Closing of a Speech

In this unit you will learn to:

- identify the functions of the opening and closing of a speech;
- understand the key elements of the opening and closing of a speech;
- explore the skills to construct the opening and closing of a speech.

5.1 Speech Reading: A Personal Journey and a Call to Action for a Paid Parental Leave

Activity 1 **Lead-in Listening**

Listen to the speech and write down the outline.

Activity 2 **Pre-reading Questions**

1. What do you know about the maternity leave? Is a 12-week maternity leave without pay enough for new moms?

2. What are the meanings of maternity, paternity and parental leave?

3. What measures do the whole society and the government take to help the parents to have babies?

A Personal Journey and a Call to Action for a Paid Parental Leave[1]

1   When I was a very young person, I began my career as an actress. Whenever my mother wasn't free to drive me into Manhattan for **auditions**, I would take the train from suburban New Jersey and meet my father—who would have left his desk at the law office where he worked—and we would meet under the Upper Platform

---

[1] This text is an excerpted speech delivered by UN Women Goodwill Ambassador Anne Hathaway at the UN Official Commemoration of International Women's Day from the Weibo website.

Arrivals and Departures sign in Penn Station. We would then get on the subway together and when we surfaced, he would ask me, "Which way is north?" I wasn't very good at finding north in the beginning, but I **auditioned** fair amount and so my Dad kept asking me, "Which way is north?" Over time, I got better at finding it.

2   I was struck by that memory yesterday while boarding the plane to come here—not just by how far my life has come since then, but by how meaningful that seemingly small lesson has been. When I was still a child, my father developed my sense of direction and now, as an adult, I trust my ability to **navigate** space. My father helped give me the confidence to guide myself through the world.

3   In late March, last year, 2016, I became a parent for the first time. I remember the indescribable—and as I understand it pretty universal—experience of holding my week-old son and feeling my priorities change **on a cellular level**. I remember I experienced a shift in consciousness that gave me the ability to maintain my love of career and also cherish something else, someone else, so much, much more. Like so many parents, I wondered how I was going to balance my work with my new role as a parent, and in that moment, I remember that the statistic for the U.S.'s policy on maternity leave[①] flashed in my mind.

4   American women are currently entitled to 12 weeks unpaid leave. American men are entitled to nothing. That information landed differently for me. When one week after my son's birth, I could barely walk. That information landed differently when I was getting to know a human who was completely dependent on my husband and I for everything, when I was dependent on my husband for most things, and when we were relearning everything we thought we knew about our family and our relationship. It landed differently.

5   Somehow, we and every American parent were expected to be "back to normal" in under three months. Without income? I remember thinking to myself, "If the practical reality of pregnancy is another mouth to feed in your home, and America is a country where most people are living **paycheck to paycheck**, how does 12 weeks unpaid leave economically work?"

6   The truth is: for too many people, it doesn't. One in four American women go back to work two weeks after giving birth because they can't afford to take off any more time than that. That is 25 percent of American women. Equally disturbing, women who can afford to take the full 12 weeks often don't, because it will mean incurring a "motherhood penalty"—meaning they will be perceived as less dedicated to their job and will be passed over for promotions and other career advancement. In my own household, my mother had to choose between a career and raising three children—a choice that left her unpaid and underappreciated as a homemaker—because there just wasn't support for both paths…

7   The deeper into the issue of paid parental leave I go, the clearer I see the connection between persisting barriers to women's full equality and empowerment, and the need to redefine and in some cases, **destigmatize** men's role as caregivers. In other words, in order to liberate women, we need to liberate men.

8   The assumption and common practice that women and girls look after the home and the family are a stubborn and very real stereotype that not only discriminates against women, but limits men's participation and connection within the family and society. These limitations have broad-ranging and significant effects for them and for the children. We know this. So why do we continue to undervalue fathers and overburden mothers?

...

9   Along with UN Women[②], I am issuing a call to action for countries, companies and institutions globally to step up and become champions for paid parental leave. In 2013, provisions for paid parental leave were in only 66 countries out of 190 UN member states. I look forward to beginning with the UN itself which has not yet achieved **parity** and whose paid parental leave policies are currently up for review. Let us lead by example in creating a world in which women and men are not economically punished for wanting to be parents.

...

10   Every generation must find their north. When women around the world demanded the right to vote, we took a fundamental step towards equality. North. When same-sex marriage was passed in the U.S., we put an end to a discriminatory law. North. When millions of men and boys, and prime ministers, and deputy directors of the UN, the President of the General Assembly... When men in this room and around the world—the ones we cannot see, the ones who support us in ways we cannot know but we feel—when they answered Emma Watson's call to be HeForShe[③], the world grew. North.

11   We must ask ourselves, how will we be more tomorrow than we are today? The whole world grows when people like you and me take a stand, because we know that beyond the idea of how women and men are different, there is a deeper truth that love is love, and parents are parents.

> **Analysis**
>
> In the speech, Anne Hathaway raises the question of parity. By describing the current tough situations for women with pregnancy and with newly-born babies, she exemplifies difficult choices women have to face due to the inequality concerning gender issues.

Instead of asking for help for women directly, she points out how essential a paid parental leave should be. Hence, giving men paternity leave is a must. Being a parent means a lot of things, and spending time with the kids will be significant for children's growth. She finally concludes by reviewing the metaphorical meaning of "North" in people's lives, not just for citizens, but also for governments, companies and institutions.

The speech begins with a little story of her father and herself leading tactically to the idea of finding the right direction "North" in doing things. This is an attractive opening of the speech since one of the main purposes of the introductory part is to gain the audience's attention and interest. The story is quite personal so that it might involve the audience immediately since everyone could have a conversation with parents like that. Besides, a second purpose has also been achieved—it predicts and leads to the main body. In addition, the central word "North" plays as a cue word and is referred back to by the closing of the speech.

Useful Words & Expressions

audition	*n./v.*	试演，试镜
destigmatize	*v.*	消除……的偏见
navigate	*v.*	导航，领航；（船只）航行
parity	*n.*	（尤指薪金或地位）平等，相同
live paycheck to paycheck		月光族
on a cellular level		从根本上

Notes

① maternity leave: It refers to the time off taken by a mother. In this speech, Anne Hathaway mentioned a third usage, "parental leave", which can be understood as the leave for child-rearing and does not specify gender, applicable to either parent.

② UN Women: It is the United Nations entity for gender equality and the empowerment of women, which has its headquarters in New York. Its office in China focuses on promoting women's development and safeguarding women's rights.

③ HeForShe: Also known as the HeForShe Solidarity Movement, it is a solidarity campaign initiated by UN Women. The campaign was launched by actress Emma Watson in her speech at the United Nations on September 20, 2014. The movement aims to call on everyone—including men—to oppose all forms of unfair treatment faced by women, to participate in action, and to bring about change.

Critical Thinking

1. Why are the opening and closing of a speech considered crucial components of a speech, and how do they influence the audience's perception and retention of the speech?
2. What are some effective strategies for crafting the opening of a speech that engages the audience and sets the stage for the speech's main content?
3. How can a speaker create the closing of a speech that effectively summarizes the speech and leaves a lasting impression on the audience?
4. What challenges do novice public speakers commonly face when crafting the opening and closing of a speech, and how can these challenges be overcome?
5. How can speaker balance creativity with structure in the opening and closing of a speech, particularly when discussing topics like "A Personal Journey and a Call to Action for Paid Parental Leave"?

5.2 Skill Focus: Opening and Closing of a Speech

A speech needs the clearly defined opening and closing. These two help the audience to see what's to come in the speech, and then let them mentally prepare for the end. But the problem for most novice public speakers is quite obvious: They just don't know how to begin and end their speeches. In this unit, why the opening and closing of a speech are important will be explored, and various ways you can use to create the impactful opening and closing of a speech will be identified.

5.2.1 Opening of a Speech

Although the opening of a speech fulfills many functions, it is not the main part of a speech. Therefore, it should be relatively short and stick to the point. In most cases, the opening of a speech serves for the following four purposes: (1) to get the audience's attention and interest; (2) to establish credibility; (3) to create a positive relationship with the audience; (4) to preview the body of the speech. Generally the opening of a speech will only be about 10%–20% of the total speech.

1. Get the Audience's Attention and Interest

People form opinions quickly. That's why the opening of a speech matters. A novice speaker always assumes that people will naturally listen because someone is speaking. But the truth is if you can't get the audience's attention in the first few words, they are likely to be distracted by many other things: the thoughts in their heads, the smartphones in their pockets, and so on. Then they may never pay attention to the content of your speech. To get the audience's attention and keep them interested, the following methods can be taken to make your speech fascinating.

1) Relate the Topic to the Audience

Generally speaking, people are more interested in things that have direct impact on them. If you can relate your topic to the audience, they will pay more attention to your speech. Make sure to open your speech with something that can make your audience feel involved.

> **Example**
>
> I have a confession to make, but first, I want you to make a little confession to me, if you have experienced relatively little stress. Anyone? How about a moderate amount of stress? Who has experienced a lot of stress? (How to Make Stress Your Friend, Kelly McGonigal)

2) State the Importance of Your Topic

Your topic is so important that it deserves a public speech, and you should make your audience know it. So it's essential to illustrate the importance of the topic to your audience. Knowing the details of the important issue can make the audience more concerned about your speech.

3) Startle the Audience

It's highly effective to startle the audience with shocking or unexpected remarks so that their attention will be drawn to the topic immediately. These remarks usually involve startling statements, statistics, or facts. There's one point that you should be clear about: These startling remarks must be in consistency with your topic. Otherwise the audience will be confused or even annoyed. Compared with statements or facts, startling statistics work wonders so directly that they catch attention and arouse the audience's curiosity to listen further for "What's next?" or "What's the rest of the story?".

> **Example**
>
> Okay, now I don't want to alarm anybody in this room, but it just comes to my attention that the person to your right is a liar. (Laughter) Also, the person to your left is a liar. Also the person sitting in your very seat is a liar. We're all liars. (How to Spot a Liar, Pamela Meyer)

There's something you should care about startling the audience: (1) make sure the source is reliable and accurate; (2) make sure the statistics or facts are suitable for your context; (3) startling remarks should be followed by your own context. Put the remarks into the suitable context immediately.

4) Arouse the Curiosity of the Audience

To make your speech compelling, you can open your speech with a chain of rhetorical questions to hook the audience.

> **Example**
>
> You talk about the history of the Spring Festival. The speech may begin by asking the audience, "Did you go back to your hometown in the last Spring Festival for a family reunion?". In this case, you do not expect the audience to shout out an answer, but rather to think about the question as the speech goes on. In doing so, the question arouses the audience's curiosity about when the family reunion became a ritual for the holiday. Also it instantly relates the topic of the traditions of the Spring Festival to the audience themselves.

5) Use a Quotation

Quotation is a great way to start a speech and capture the audience's attention. Quotes can just take up valuable space where you can put content unless they are not properly used. So a quote should get to the point quickly. And you should be sure to use the quote purposefully and not just as placeholders. Be sure to give the source first so that it isn't mistaken as your own wording. And try not to go for overused quotes. Instead, you can go for an equally excellent but less quoted one.

> **Examples**
>
> (1) There's only one heroism in the world: to see the world as it is, and to love it.
>
> (2) No one ever reads a book. He reads himself through books.

Although quotation is a good attention-getter, don't forget to follow these principles: (1) it's not sufficient to only copy the sentences and you should make sure you place the quotation in the context of your speech properly so that it will work effectively; (2) don't get too lazy to start every speech with a quote; (3) don't use extremely long quotations (three or more sentences), because this is just a part of the introduction. You are not making a point.

6) Tell a Story

Telling a story is another powerful way to get the audience's attention. A well-told story will allow the audience to "see" things in their mind and to join your emotions. Be sure to give a very brief story at the beginning with a clear point.

> **Example**
>
> As in the previous sample speech delivered by Anne Hathaway, she told a story between her father and herself on the issue of finding a direction. This is an everyday conversation that not only relates to the audience immediately but also previews the topic of guiding her through the world. When the cue word "North" has been mentioned multiple times, she perfectly ends the speech with a strong connection with the central idea of the speech.

2. Establish Credibility

After you get the audience's attention and interest with a hook or attention-grabber, you are supposed to let the audience know you are a knowledgeable and credible source of information you are going to share. Whether you are informing, persuading or entertaining the audience, your credibility lets them know you are qualified to speak on the topic. Walk through a possible credibility checklist before your speech writing: credentials, qualifications, training, classes, or research will all contribute to establishing or enhancing your credibility.

> **Example**
>
> I started studying resilience research a decade ago at the University of Pennsylvania in Philadelphia. It was an amazing time to be there because the professors who trained me had just picked up the contract to train all 1.1 million American soldiers to be as mentally fit as they always have been physically fit. (The Three Secrets of Resilient People, Lucy Hone)

3. Create a Positive Relationship with the Audience

The positive speaker-audience relationship plays an important role in a speech. In the opening of a speech, you may want to explain to your audience why you are giving them this information. You can make a connection through this shared information and explain to them how it will benefit them. If the topic is a controversial or less-supported one, this positive relationship is crucial for the success of your speech.

4. Preview the Body of the Speech

As you introduce the fundamentals of your speech in the introduction part, the audience will be aware of the purpose of your speech as well as the main points. For most speeches, the preview should come at the end of the introduction. Previewing your main points helps the audience to know what to expect and get themselves prepared for your speech. Your preview should be simple, concise and easy to follow so that there won't be anything confusing for the audience.

> **Example**
>
> Today in your discussion of Stephen Hawking, you will look at his birth and early years, his theory and contribution to physics, and his illness and death.

Start your speech in a creative way so that it can help to get the audience's attention. Don't rush to speak and wait for the audience to settle down and focus on you. Keep the four major functions of the opening of the speech and the tips in mind and your speech is more likely to be an impressive one.

5.2.2 Closing of a Speech

The closing of a speech is the last statement you will share with the audience. In order to make it as strong and memorable as possible, the closing of a speech can recap main points, restate the central idea or the thesis, and leave the audience with something to consider. Generally, there are two major elements a conclusion should cover: signaling the end of the speech, and reinforcing the central idea.

1. Signaling the End of a Speech

Just like the opening of a speech prepares the audience what to expect, the closing of a speech will prepare the audience for the closing of the speech. The first few words of your speech make the audience want to listen and the last few sentences help them to decide how they feel about you and your speech. In a way, signaling the end gives the audience time to begin mentally organizing and cataloging all the points you have made for further consideration later.

There are several ways to signal the end of a speech. You may either signal the audience with obvious cue words such as "in conclusion", or you can signal them in the sight by changing your manner of delivery. This is usually achieved through the change of the tone, pacing, intonation, and rhythm of your voice.

2. Reinforcing the Central Idea

Unlike a paper where the reader can reread the words as many times as they want, an oral communication gives only one opportunity for the audience to catch and remember the points you have talked about in it. Thus reviewing the main points in the closing of a speech, you can increase the likelihood that the audience will understand and retain your main points after the speech is over.

Since you are trying to close the speech, do remember that no new material or ideas enter the conclusion part. If you say something like "There are still several issues important but I am not going to talk about them today.", then it will leave the audience not just confused but also doubtful about why you fail to address them in the body part if those issues are important and they even question your credibility. As for a persuasive speech, it's extremely important not to include any counter-argument in the end.

You could use one of the following common ways to reinforce the central idea: (1) to summarize your speech; (2) to end your speech with a quotation; (3) to make a dramatic statement; (4) to refer to the introduction.

Example 1

There's a wonderful quote from Benjamin Franklin, "There are three sorts of people in the world: Those who are immovable, people who don't get it, or don't want to do anything about it; there are people who are movable, people who see the need for change and are prepared to listen to it; there are people who move, people who make things happen." And if we can encourage more people, that will be a movement. And if the movement is strong enough, that's, in the best sense of the word, a revolution. And that's what we need. (How to Escape Education's Death Valley, Sir Ken Robinson)

Example 2

Your families, your teachers, and I are doing everything we can to make sure you have the education you need to answer these questions. I'm working hard to fix up your classrooms and get you the books and the equipment and the computers you need to learn. But you've got to do your part, too. So I expect all of you to get serious this year. I expect you to put your best effort into everything you do. I expect great things from each of you. So don't let us down. Don't let your family down or your country down. Most of all, don't let yourself down. Make us all proud. (Remarks by President Barrack Obama, addressed to school children at Wakefield High School)

Exercises

Choose the best options to answer the following questions or fill in the blanks according to the information given in this unit.

1. Which of the following is NOT true?
    A. The opening of a speech should preview what you are going to talk about.

B. Public speakers always know how to start their speech in a smart way.

C. The closing of a speech should be able to provide some key takeaways for the audience.

D. In order to have creative speeches, a public speaker should go through the process of doing research and organizing ideas.

2. Generally speaking, the opening of a speech should be no more than _____ of the length of your speech.

   A. 3%–5%   B. 5%–10%
   C. 10%–15%   D. 10%–20%

3. Which of the following is NOT a method to get the audience's attention and interest?

   A. Startle the audience.
   B. Use a quotation.
   C. Establish credibility.
   D. Tell a story.

4. Which of the following will decrease your credibility?

   A. Use irrelevant statistics or facts.
   B. Provide a reliable and accurate source.
   C. Guarantee the startling remarks suitable for your context.
   D. Put startling remarks into your context.

5. Which of the following is one of the ways to restate the central idea in the closing of a speech?

   A. Give more examples.
   B. Tell the audience what you fail to mention in the speech.
   C. Refer back to the introduction.
   D. Change the tone of your voice.

6. Which of the following is one of the four major objectives of the opening of a speech?

   A. To reveal the topic.
   B. To call on an action.
   C. To reinforce the central idea.
   D. To identify the audience.

7. Which will go first when you prepare for the speech writing?

   A. Telling a story.
   B. Preparing the body.
   C. Beginning with a quotation.

D. Preparing the introduction.

8. Which of the following would you most likely find in the opening of a speech?
   A. An outline statement.
   B. A credibility statement.
   C. A causal argument.
   D. A transitional statement.

9. The best time to work out the exact wording of the opening of a speech is _____.
   A. shortly after you determine the central idea
   B. after you prepare the body of the speech
   C. before you work out the conclusion
   D. when you prepare your speaking outline

10. Read the following sentence from a speech introduction carefully. This is an example of a _____.
    In my speech today, I will show you the serious health dangers posed by the flu, and I will urge each of you to get a flu shot every year without fail.
    A. transition statement
    B. credibility statement
    C. preview statement
    D. summary statement

11. Which of the following can be used as a means of reinforcing the central idea in the closing of a speech?
    A. End with a touching story.
    B. End with a quotation.
    C. End with showing gratitude and respect.
    D. End with apologizing for not covering enough details.

12. Which of the following would you most likely find in the closing of a speech?
    A. A preview statement.
    B. A startling number to arouse curiosity.
    C. A restatement of the central idea.
    D. A credibility statement.

13. When you start a speech by saying "Laughter is a good medicine.", you use a method of _____.
    A. startling the audience
    B. beginning with a quotation
    C. stating the importance of your topic

D. relating the topic to the audience

14. Which of the following is unlikely to be found in the closing of a speech?

    A. A reference to the introduction.

    B. A call on the audience to take action.

    C. Statement to arouse curiosity.

    D. Inspirational words.

15. Referring back to your introduction in the closing of your speech is recommended as a way to _____.

    A. develop a dissolve ending

    B. secure the audience's attention

    C. move the audience to action

    D. give the speech psychological unity

16. If the closing of a speech is a dramatic quotation that summarizes the central idea while referring to the introduction, a speaker uses _____ in the conclusion.

    A. one skill

    B. two skills

    C. three skills

    D. four skills

17. In preparing the closing of a speech, you should _____.

    A. not leave anything in your conclusion to chance

    B. conclude with a bang, not a whimper

    C. not be long winded

    D. do all of the above

18. Which of the following methods is NOT contained in signaling the closing of your speech?

    A. To change your voice.

    B. To fade steps by steps.

    C. To apologize to the audience.

    D. To say "In conclusion".

19. Which statement about the closing of a speech is TRUE?

    A. The closing of a speech will linger your final impression in the audience's minds.

    B. The closing of a speech is the last chance you can build up credibility.

    C. You need to craft your gratitude to the audience with much care.

    D. You should provide counter-argument to achieve a thorough understanding for the audience.

20. All of the following are common techniques used in the closing of a speech EXCEPT
    _____.
    A. summarizing the speech
    B. ending with a quotation
    C. making a long-winded statement
    D. referring to the introduction

5.3 Speaking Task: Making a Speech on an Unforgettable Person

Task Make a speech on an unforgettable person in 150 words. You may choose either one of the following sets of keywords to describe Person A or B. Make sure your speech sticks to the same order of the occurrence of the words.

Person A: critical, stubborn, reckless, industrious, intelligent

Person B: intelligent, industrious, reckless, stubborn, critical

5.4 Self-Reflection: Evaluating the Opening and Closing of Your Speech

Evaluate your speech based on how well you meet each specific criterion. Rate your speech on each point: E—excellent, G—good, A—average, F—fair, P—poor.

Checklist: The Opening and Closing of Your Speech

Items	Scores					Comments
	E	G	A	F	P	
Introduction						
To gain attention and interest						
To introduce topic clearly						
To relate topic to audience						
To establish credibility						

(To be continued)

(Continued)

Items	Scores					Comments
	E	G	A	F	P	
Body						
Main points clear						
Main points fully supported						
Organization well planned						
Language clear and appropriate						
Connectives effective						
Conclusion						
Preparing audience for ending						
Reinforcing central idea						
Vivid ending						
Delivery						
Maintain strong eye contact						
Avoid distracting mannerisms						
Articulate words clearly						
Use vocal variety to add impact						
Use pause effectively						

Unit 6

Speaking to Inform

In this unit you will learn to:

- choose an informative speech topic;
- prepare a good outline for an informative speech;
- follow the proven guidelines to deliver an informative speech.

6.1 Speech Reading: The Chinese Dream of the Great Renewal

Activity 1 Lead-in Listening

Listen to the speech and write down the multiple definitions of a smart city.

A smart city _____

A smart city _____

Activity 2 Pre-reading Questions

1. What is the Chinese dream? How is it different from the American Dream?

2. Who put forward the notion of "the Chinese Dream of the great renewal" and under what circumstances?

3. How do you understand the word "renewal" in "the Chinese Dream of the great renewal"?

The Chinese Dream of the Great Renewal[1]

1   The ocean is vast for it refuses no rivers. All civilizations are **crystallizations** of mankind's hard work and wisdom. Every civilization is unique.

   ...

---

1 This text is adapted from President Xi Jinping's speech at UNESCO from the Chinadaily website.

2   Having gone through over 5,000 years of **vicissitudes**, the Chinese civilization has always kept to its original root. Unique in representing China spiritually, it contains some most profound pursuits of the Chinese nation and provides it with abundant **nourishment** for existence and development. Though born on the soil of China, it has come to its present form through constant exchanges and mutual learning with other civilizations.

3   In the 2nd century B.C., China began working on the Silk Road leading to the Western Regions. In 138 B.C. and 119 B.C., **Envoy** Zhang Qian[①] of the Han Dynasty made two trips to those regions, spreading the Chinese culture there and bringing into China grape, **alfalfa**, **pomegranate**, **flax**, **sesame** and other products. In the Western Han Dynasty, China's **merchant** fleets sailed as far as India and Sri Lanka where they traded China's silk for colored glaze, pearls and other products. The Tang Dynasty saw dynamic interactions between China and other countries. According to historical documents, the dynasty exchanged envoys with over 70 countries, and Chang'an, the capital of Tang, **bustled** with envoys, merchants and students from other countries. Exchanges of such a **magnitude** helped the spread of the Chinese culture to the rest of the world and the introduction into China of the cultures and products from other countries. In the early 15th century, Zheng He[②], the famous navigator of China's Ming Dynasty, made seven **expeditions** to the Western Seas, reaching many Southeast Asian countries and even Kenya on the east coast of Africa. These trips left behind many stories of friendly exchanges between the people of China and countries along the route. In late Ming Dynasty and early Qing Dynasty, the Chinese people began to learn modern science and technology with great **zeal**, as the European knowledge of **astronomy**, medicine, mathematics, geometry and geography were being introduced into China, which helped **broaden the horizon** of the Chinese people. Thereafter, exchanges and mutual learning between the Chinese civilization and other civilizations became more frequent. There were indeed conflicts, **frictions**, **bewilderment** and denial in this process. But the more dominant features of the period were learning, **digestion**, integration and innovation.

...

4   The Chinese people are striving to fulfill the Chinese dream of the great renewal of the Chinese nation. The Chinese dream of the great renewal of the Chinese nation is about prosperity of the country, **rejuvenation** of the nation, and happiness of the people. It reflects the ideal of the Chinese people of today as well as the fine tradition of **relentlessly** seeking progress that we have had since ancient times.

...

5　A civilization carries on its back the soul of a country or nation. It needs to be passed on from one generation to the next. Yet more importantly, it needs to **keep pace with** the times and innovate with courage. As we pursue the Chinese dream, the Chinese people will encourage creative shifts and innovative development of the Chinese civilization in keeping with the progress of the times. We need to inject new vitality into the Chinese civilization by energizing all cultural elements that transcend time, space and national borders and that possess both perpetual appeal and current value, and we need to **bring** all collections in our museums, all heritage structures across our lands and all records in our classics **to life**. In this way, the Chinese civilization, together with the rich and colorful civilizations created by the people of other countries, will provide mankind with the right cultural guidance and strong motivation.

Analysis

This speech offers a comprehensive overview of the Chinese civilization and its interactions with other civilizations. President Xi Jinping highlights how, despite its vastness, the Chinese civilization has maintained its unique essence and rich history. He also emphasizes how the Chinese civilization has evolved through exchanges and mutual learning with other civilizations, contributing to the spread of Chinese culture and the introduction of foreign cultures into China.

The speech delves into several significant historical events that demonstrate the dynamic nature of the Chinese civilization, such as the Silk Road, expeditions by Zheng He, and the introduction of modern science and technology during the Ming and Qing Dynasties. While acknowledging the challenges and contradictions that accompanied these exchanges, the presenter underscores the dominant features of this period: learning, digestion, integration, and innovation.

The Chinese dream of the great renewal of the nation is a central theme of the speech, representing the prosperity, rejuvenation, and happiness of the Chinese people. The presenter stresses that realizing this dream is a process of material and cultural development, which requires both preserving the soul of the country and adapting to changing times through courageous innovation.

To achieve this, the presenter advocates for the reinvigoration of all cultural elements that transcend time, space, and national borders. By doing so, he believes that the Chinese civilization, along with the diverse civilizations of other countries, can provide humanity with the right cultural guidance and strong motivation for progress.

Useful Words & Expressions

alfalfa	n.	苜蓿
astronomy	n.	天文学
bewilderment	n.	困惑
bustle	v.	奔忙；繁忙，热闹
crystallization	n.	结晶化；具体化
digestion	n.	消化
envoy	n.	使者，使节
expedition	n.	远征；考察
flax	n.	亚麻
friction	n.	摩擦，不合
magnitude	n.	（巨大的）规模
merchant	n.	商人
nourishment	n.	养分；滋养品
pomegranate	n.	石榴
rejuvenation	n.	恢复青春
relentlessly	adv.	不屈不挠地
renewal	n.	恢复；复兴
sesame	n.	芝麻
vicissitude	n.	变迁
zeal	n.	热忱
bring... to life		让……焕发生机
broaden the horizon (of...)		拓宽（……的）视野
keep pace with...		跟上……的步伐

Notes

① Zhang Qian (circa 164 B.C.E.–114 B.C.E.): He was an outstanding diplomat, traveler, and explorer of the Han Dynasty in China. He was also the pioneer of the Silk Road. His hometown is located in Bowang Village, 2 kilometers south of Chenggu County in Hanzhong City, Shaanxi Province, by the Han River.

② Zheng He (1371–1433): He was a eunuch, navigator, and diplomat of the Ming Dynasty in China. In the second year of the Yongle Era (1404), Zheng He achieved remarkable military merits. The Yongle Emperor, Zhu Di, bestowed the surname "Zheng" upon Ma He in Nanjing as a commemoration of his achievements. Hence he is historically known as "Zheng He". He was promoted to the position of a high-ranking eunuch in charge of the Imperial Household Department, with a rank of fourth grade, a status second only to the Director of the Imperial Secretariat. Between 1405 and 1433, Zheng He made seven voyages to the Western Seas, accomplishing a great feat in human history.

Critical Thinking

1. What are the key characteristics of an effective informative speech, and how can a speaker ensure that his or her speech is both informative and engaging?
2. How can a speaker effectively convey complex information in an informative speech without overwhelming the audience?
3. What role does the audience analysis play in the preparation of an informative speech? How can a speaker tailor his or her content to meet the audience's needs and expectations?
4. How can a speaker evaluate the effectiveness of his or her informative speech, and what strategies can be used for improvement?
5. After reading "The Chinese Dream of the Great Renewal", how can an informative speech be crafted to convey the knowledge and aspirations of the dream, and what key elements should be included to ensure that the speech educates the audience about its significance and implications for both China and the global community?

6.2 Skill Focus: Speaking to Inform

An informative speech can be described as a speech based totally, absolutely, and solely on facts and its main purpose is to inform rather than to persuade, to amuse, or to inspire. Basically, an informative speech conveys knowledge, a mission that every character engages in each day in various shapes or forms. Whether giving a person who's misplaced using directions, explaining the specials of the day as a server, or describing the plot of a film to friends, people interact in varieties of informative speeches.

6.2.1 Choosing a Focused Informative Speech Topic

A good informative speech can have a significant impact on the audience, whether it's inspiring them to take action or informing them about important issues. Choosing the right topic is crucial to deliver an effective informative speech.

Here are tips for picking a focused and relevant informative speech topic.

(1) Identify your area of expertise or interest. Choose a topic that you are knowledgeable and passionate about. This can allow you to provide valuable insights and engage with your audience.

(2) Consider current events or trends. Look for topics that are relevant to current events or trends in your community, which can help you to stay up-to-date and provide fresh perspectives on familiar issues.

(3) Choose a topic that resonates with your audience. Think about the interests and concerns of the audience and choose a topic that appeal to them. This can help you to connect with the audience on a personal level and keep their attention throughout your speech.

(4) Consider the scope of your topic. Determine how broad or narrow you want to make your topic. A broad topic may require more research and preparation, while a narrow topic may be easier to structure and deliver.

(5) Think about the format of your speech. Consider how you want to structure your speech and what type of information you want to include. This can help you to determine which topic is best suited for your delivery style.

(6) Ask for feedback. Share your ideas with friends, family, or colleagues and ask for their input. They may provide valuable insights or suggestions that you don't considered.

(7) Keep it simple. Choose a topic that is easy to understand, which makes it easier for the audience to follow along and retain the information you are presenting.

By following these tips, you can pick a focused informative speech topic that will engage your audience, inform them, and leave a lasting impression. Remember to choose a topic that you are passionate about and that aligns with your values and goals as a speaker.

6.2.2 Avoiding Faux or Fake Informative Speech Topics

Choosing a topic for an informative speech can be a daunting task, especially when you want to make sure that your message is clear and effective. However, it's important to avoid faux or fake informative speech topics that may misinform the audience or detract from the overall impact of your speech.

Here are tips for avoiding such topics.

(1) Avoid using buzzwords or jargon. Avoid using terms or phrases that are specific to a particular industry or field without providing context or explanation. This can make your speech seem unprofessional or confusing.

(2) Don't rely on hearsay or rumors. Avoid using information that is not supported by credible sources or that has been widely discredited. This can make your speech seem untrustworthy and unreliable.

(3) Avoid sensationalism or exaggeration. Avoid making exaggerated claims or using hyperbole to grab your audience's attention. This can make your speech seem insincere and unprofessional.

(4) Avoid using personal anecdotes without context. Personal anecdotes can be a powerful way to engage your audience, but you should make sure they are relevant to your topic and provide context for the information you are presenting.

(5) Avoid using humor without caution. Humor can be a great way to break the ice and engage your audience, but make sure it is appropriate and doesn't detract from the overall message of your speech.

(6) Avoid using overly simplistic language. Avoid using overly simplistic language that may be difficult for the audience to understand. Use clear and concise language that is easy to follow.

(7) Avoid relying on pop culture references. Pop culture references can be entertaining, but they may not be relevant to the audience or may not provide valuable insights into your topic.

By following these tips, you can avoid faux or fake informative speech topics that may misinform your audience or detract from the overall impact of your speech.

6.2.3 Writing an Informative Speech Outline

Most speakers and audience members would agree that a well-organized informative speech is easier to deliver. Public speaking instructors, in particular, believe in the power of organization, which is why they encourage (and frequently require) the speaker to write an outline for the speech. Outlines, or textual arrangements of all the various elements of a speech, are popular ways to organize a speech before the speech is delivered. Most extemporaneous speakers keep their outlines with them during the speech to ensure that no important elements are missed and to keep them on track. Writing an outline is also helpful in the speech writing process because it forces the speaker to consider the main points and sub-points, the examples they want to include, and how these elements relate to one another. In short, the outline serves as both an organizational tool and a guide for delivering a speech.

> **Outline Formatting Guide**
> Title:
> Topic:

Specific Purpose Statement:

Thesis Statement:

Introduction

Attention Getter

Topic/Audience Relevance

Establish Your Credibility

Central Idea / Thesis Statement

Preview Main Points

(Transition)

Body

I. Main Point 1

A. First Sub-point

1. Support

2. Support

B. Second Sub-point

1. Support

2. Support

(Transition)

II. Main Point 2

A. First Sub-point

1. Support

2. Support

3. Support

B. Second Sub-point

1. Support

2. Support

3. Support

(Transition)

Conclusion

Summary

Provide Closure

Clincher

1. Writing a Preparation Outline for an Informative Speech

The preparation outline, also known as a working, practice, or rough outline, is used to work through the various components of your speech in an inventive format. When writing the preparation outline, you should concentrate on finalizing the purpose and thesis statements, logically ordering your main points, deciding where to include supporting material, and refining the overall organizational pattern of your speech. You may need to rearrange your points and add or remove supporting points as you write the preparation outline. You may also notice that some of your main points are adequately supported while others are not. The final draft of your preparation outline should include complete sentences that comprise a complete script of the speech. However, in most cases, the preparation outline is only used for planning and is translated into a speaking outline before you deliver the speech.

At the top of the outline are the title, topic, specific purpose statement, and thesis statement. These elements are beneficial because they remind you of what you are attempting to accomplish in your speech. They also benefit anyone reading and viewing your sketch, because knowing what you want to achieve will determine how they perceive the elements of your sketch. Also, write down transition statements that you'll use to remind your audience of what you're transitioning from one point to another. They appear in parentheses among the main points.

> **Example**
>
> Title: The Art and Science of Playing the Guitar
>
> Specific Purpose
>
> Thesis Statement
>
> I. Introduction
>
> A. Definition of guitar and its significance in music history
>
> B. Importance of understanding the technical aspects of playing the guitar
>
> C. Overview of the speech's structure and key points
>
> (Transition)
>
> II. History of the Guitar
>
> Origin and development of the guitar
>
> 1. Early instruments and their evolution into modern guitars
>
> 2. Cultural influences on guitar design and style
>
> (Transition)

III. Technical Elements of Guitar Playing

A. Finger-picking techniques and finger placement

1. Different approaches to finger-picking and the benefits

1) Different approaches to finger-picking:

- Alternate picking: This approach involves picking the strings in alternate patterns, such as up and down or left and right. It can produce a crisp, clear sound and is often used in rock and folk music.

- Flat-picking: This approach involves using a flat pick instead of a finger pick to strum the strings. It can create a more mellow, acoustic sound and is often used in blues and country music.

- Plucking: This approach involves plucking the strings with the tips of the fingers instead of using a pick. It can produce a more percussive sound and is often used in classical and jazz music.

2) Benefits of different approaches to finger-picking: Each approach has its own unique sound and can be used to achieve different effects in a song. By experimenting with different techniques, musicians can find the approach that best suits their style and musical goals.

2. Tips for improving finger-picking skills

- Practice regularly: Like any skill, finger-picking needs much practice. Set aside time each day to practice and focus on specific aspects that need improvement.

- Start with simple chords: Begin by learning basic chord progressions and practicing finger-picking along with them. As you become more comfortable, move on to more complex songs and techniques.

- Use a metronome: A metronome can help you to develop your timing and accuracy when playing finger-picking. Start at a slow tempo and gradually increase the speed as you become more confident.

- Listen carefully: Pay attention to the sounds you are producing and try to identify the aspects which you can improve. Experiment with different techniques and see what works best for you.

- Stay relaxed: Tension in the hands and wrists can make it difficult to play finger-picking accurately. Take breaks if you feel tension, and practice relaxation like deep breathing or meditation.

B. Chord progressions and song structure

1. Common chord progressions used in popular music

2. Techniques for creating interesting and dynamic song structures

C. Music theory and ear training

1. Understanding musical notation and scales

2. Techniques for developing a better ear for music

(Transition)

IV. Creative Strategies for Guitar Playing

A. Improvisation techniques and exercises

1. Ways to develop improvisational skills and creativity

2. Examples of famous guitarists who excel at improvisation

B. Collaboration with other musicians

Approaches to working with other instruments and vocalists in a band or ensemble

C. Personal expression through guitar playing

How to find your own voice as a musician and express yourself through your playing

(Transition)

V. Conclusion

A. Recap of key points discussed throughout the speech

B. Emphasis on the importance of mastering the technical aspects of playing the guitar to become a skilled musician

C. Call to action for exploring the art and science of playing the guitar further

2. Writing a Speaking Outline for an Informative Speech

The advantages of writing a speaking outline are: to help you to organize the content of your speech; to create two contours for a successful voice-over; to help you to prepare for your presentation. The following are some tips for writing a speaking outline for an informative speech: (1) ensure that the text is legible by writing large enough so that you do not have to bring the cards or pages close to your eyes to read them; (2) verify that the cards or pages are in the correct order and bound together in a way that prevents them from becoming disorganized; (3) in case the cards or pages do become disorganized, be sure to number each one in the top right corner so that you can quickly and easily reorganize them; (4) avoid fidgeting with the cards or pages while speaking. It is best to lay them down if you have a podium or table in front of you, but not, practice speaking more so that you can quickly look down, read the text, and then return your gaze to the audience.

> **Example**
>
> Title: The Psychological Effects of Using Social Media
>
> Specific Purpose
>
> Thesis Statement
>
> I. Introduction
>
> A. Definition of social media and its prevalence
>
> B. Importance of understanding the psychological effects of social media use
>
> C. Overview of the speech's structure and key points
>
> II. Positive Psychological Effects of Social Media
>
> A. Facilitating connections and relationships
>
> 1. Increased opportunities for networking and collaboration
>
> 2. Enhanced the sense of community belonging
>
> B. Boosting self-esteem and confidence
>
> 1. Sharing achievements and experiences with a supportive audience
>
> 2. Receiving positive feedback and validation from peers
>
> C. Enhancing mental well-being through mindfulness and relaxation techniques
>
> 1. Access to educational resources, such as meditation and stress management tools
>
> 2. Opportunities for virtual support groups and online therapy sessions
>
> (Transition)
>
> III. Negative Psychological Effects of Social Media
>
> A. Increasing feelings of loneliness and isolation
>
> 1. Comparison trap leading to envy and dissatisfaction with one's life
>
> 2. Reduced face-to-face interactions contributing to social disconnection
>
> B. Compromising sleep quality and overall health
>
> 1. Overuse of technology causing disrupted sleep patterns and insomnia
>
> 2. Increased exposure to blue light emitted by screens negatively impacting sleep hygiene
>
> C. Promoting unrealistic expectations and body image issues
>
> 1. Constant exposure to unattainable lifestyle leading to unrealistic standards for oneself and others
>
> 2. Increased risk of developing eating disorders, body dysmorphia, and other related conditions due to constant comparison with edited images and idealized portrayals of reality

(Transition)

IV. Strategies for Maximizing the Positive Effects of Social Media and Mitigating the Negative Effects

A. Mindful social media use practices

1. Setting boundaries on screen time and the frequency of use

2. Engaging in offline activities to maintain a healthy work-life balance

B. Developing a growth mindset and avoiding comparisons with others

1. Focusing on personal progress rather than comparing oneself with others' highlight reels

2. Building resilience through learning to cope with setbacks and failures in real life rather than seeking validation online

C. Seeking professional help when needed

1. Knowing when to reach out for support from mental health professionals or online resources for coping with negative emotions associated with social media use

2. Encouraging open communication about mental health concerns within families and friends to promote greater awareness and understanding of these issues

(Transition)

V. Conclusion

A. Recap of key points discussed throughout the speech

B. Emphasize the importance of understanding the complex psychological effects of social media on individuals and society as a whole

C. Call for the action for promoting responsible social media use and fostering healthier digital habits for a happier and more fulfilled life

Exercises

Decide whether the following statements are TRUE (T), FALSE (F) or NOT GIVEN (NG) according to the Skill Focus in this unit.

1. An informative speech conveys knowledge and a mission that every character engages in each day in various shapes or forms. (   )

2. A mediocre informative speech may not have a significant impact on the audience and may fail to inspire or inform them effectively. (   )

3. Choose topics that are relevant to current events or trends in your community or industry. (   )

4. Controversial topics can be interesting, but they can also be divisive and lead to

arguments. ( )

5. Don't waste time considering what information is already known about your topic; just focus on adding more information to fill in the gaps. ( )

6. A broad topic may require more research and preparation, while a narrow topic may be easier to structure and deliver. ( )

7. It's important to avoid fake or faux informative speech topics that may misinform your audience or detract them from the overall impact of your speech. ( )

8. Avoid using terms or phrases specific to a particular industry or field without providing context or explanation. ( )

9. Personal anecdotes can be a distraction from the main message of your speech and should be avoided unless they add value to your topic. ( )

10. Pop culture references are always relevant and provide valuable insights into your topic as long as they are entertaining your audience. ( )

11. The outline, or textual arrangement of all the various elements of a speech, is a popular way to organize a speech before it is delivered. ( )

12. You may need to rearrange your points or add or remove supporting material as you write the preparation outline. ( )

13. Write down transition statements that you'll use to guide your audience from one point to another. ( )

14. If the cards become disorganized, don't bother trying to reorganize them; just start over from scratch. ( )

15. The speech layout is unnecessary and only serves to distract from the content of the speech. ( )

6.3 Speaking Task: Making an Informative Speech About ChatGPT

Task Use explanation, description, comparison, and contrast to make the subject of your speech clear and interesting to the audience. The following template is for your reference.

Introduction Part
- Attention grabber (statement to grab the audience's attention and interest)

- Thesis statement

Body Part
- Points
- Sub-points

Conclusion Part

6.4 Self-Reflection: Evaluating Your Informative Speech

Evaluate your speech according to the following criteria. Rate your speech on each point: E—excellent, G—good, A—average, F—fair, P—poor.

Checklist: Informative Speech

Items	Scores					Comments
	E	G	A	F	P	
Introduction						
Gained attention and interest						
Introduced topic clearly						
Related topic to audience						
Established credibility						
Body						
Main points clear						
Main points fully supported						
Organization well planned						
Language clear and appropriate						
Connectives effective						
Conclusion						
Preparing audience for ending						
Reinforcing central idea						
Vivid ending						
Delivery						
Maintain strong eye contact						

(To be continued)

(Continued)

Items	Scores					Comments
	E	G	A	F	P	
Avoid distracting mannerism						
Articulate words clearly						
Use vocal variety to add impact						
Use pause effectively						

Unit 7

Speaking to Persuade

In this unit you will learn to:

- identify the three major types of persuasive speeches;
- employ the methods of organizing persuasive speeches;
- understand and employ the four primary methods of persuasion;
- understand and employ the effective methods of reasoning;
- identify and avoid fallacies in reasoning.

7.1 Speech Reading: Yes, We Can

Activity 1 Lead-in Listening

Listen to the speech and answer the following questions.

1. What is the goal of persuasive speaking?
2. Who are mostly likely to give a persuasive speech?
3. What are the supporting materials of a persuasive speech?
4. How can you organize the main body points in a persuasive speech?

Activity 2 Pre-reading Questions

1. What do you know about Barack Obama? Introduce him briefly.
2. From the title "Yes, We Can", what do you expect to get from the speech?
3. Do you know on what occasion Obama delivered such a speech?

Yes, We Can[1]

1   Thank you. Thank you. Well, first of all, I want to congratulate Senator Clinton on a hard-fought victory here in New Hampshire. She did an outstanding job. Give her a big round of applause.

---

1 This text is an excerpted script from Barack Obama's speech from the Songlyrics website.

2   You know, a few weeks ago, no one imagined that we'd have accomplished what we did here tonight in New Hampshire. No one could have imagined it. For most of this campaign, we were far behind. We always knew our climb would be steep. But in record numbers, you came out and you spoke up for change. And with your voices and your votes, you made it clear that at this moment, in this election, there is something happening in America.

3   There is something happening when men and women in Des Moines and Davenport, in Lebanon and Concord, come out in the snows of January to wait in lines that stretch block after block because they believe in what this country can be.

4   There is something happening when Americans who are young in age and in spirit, and who have never participated in politics before, turn out in numbers we have never seen because they know in their hearts that this time must be different.

5   There is something happening when people vote not just for the party that they belong to, but for the hopes that they hold in common. And whether we are rich or poor, black or white, Latino or Asian, and whether we hail from Iowa or New Hampshire, Nevada or South Carolina, we are ready to take this country in a fundamentally new direction. That's what's happening in America right now. Change is what's happening in America.

6   You, all of you who are here tonight, all who put so much heart and soul and work into this campaign, you can be the new majority who can lead this nation out of a long political darkness. Democrats, Independents, and Republicans who are tired of the division and distraction that has clouded Washington, who know that we can disagree without being disagreeable, who understand that, if we mobilize our voices to challenge the money and influence that's stood in our way and challenge ourselves to reach for something better, there is no problem we cannot solve. There is no destiny that we cannot fulfill.

7   Our new American majority can end the outrage of unaffordable, unavailable health care in our time. We can bring doctors and patients, workers and businesses, Democrats and Republicans together, and we can tell the drug and insurance industry that while they get a seat at the table, and they don't get to buy every chair. Not this time. Not now.

8   Our new majority can end the tax breaks for corporations that ship our jobs overseas, and put a middle-class tax cut in the pockets of working Americans who deserve it.

9   We can stop sending our children to schools with corridors of shame and start putting them on a pathway to success. We can stop talking about how great teachers are and start rewarding them for their greatness by giving them more pay and more

support. We can do this with our new majority.

10   We can **harness** the **ingenuity** of farmers and scientists, citizens and entrepreneurs to free this nation from the **tyranny** of oil and save our planet from a point of no return.

11   And when I am President of the United States, we will end this war in Iraq and bring our troops home. We will end this war in Iraq. We will bring our troops home. We will finish the job against aL Qaeda in Afghanistan. We will care for our veterans. We will restore our moral standing in the world. And we will never use 9/11 as a way to scare up votes, because it is not a tactic to win an election. It is a challenge that should unite America and the world against the common threats of the 21st century—terrorism and nuclear weapons, climate change and poverty, **genocide** and disease.

12   All of the candidates in this race share these goals. All of the candidates in this race have good ideas. And all are patriots who serve this country honorably. But the reason our campaign has always been different, the reason we began this improbable journey almost a year ago is because it's not just about what I will do as president. It is also about what you, the people who love this country, the citizens of the United States of America, can do to change it. That's what this election is all about. That's why tonight belongs to you.

13   It belongs to the organizers and the volunteers and the staff who believed in this journey and rallied so many others to join the cause. We know the battle ahead will be long, but always remember that no matter what obstacles stand in our way, nothing can stand in the way of the power of millions of voices calling for change.

14   We have been told we cannot do this by a chorus of **cynics**, and they will only grow louder and more **dissonant** in the weeks and months to come. We've been asked to pause for a reality check. We've been warned against offering the people of this nation false hope.

15   But in the unlikely story that is America, there has never been anything false about hope. For when we have faced down impossible odds, and when we've been told we're not ready, or that we shouldn't try, or that we can't, generations of Americans have responded with a simple creed that sums up the spirit of a people: Yes, we can. Yes, we can. Yes, we can.

16   It was a creed written into the founding documents that declared the destiny of a nation. Yes, we can.

17   It was whispered by slaves and **abolitionists** as they blazed a trail towards freedom through the darkest of nights. Yes, we can.

18   It was sung by immigrants as they struck out from distant shores, and pioneers

who pushed westward against an unforgiving wilderness. Yes, we can.

19   It was the call of workers who organized, women who reached for the **ballot**, a president who chose the moon as our new frontier, and a King who took us to the mountain top and pointed the way to the Promised Land. Yes, we can, to justice and equality. Yes, we can to opportunity and prosperity. Yes, we can heal this nation. Yes, we can repair this world. Yes, we can.

20   And so tomorrow, as we take the campaign south and west, as we learn that the struggles of the textile workers in Spartanburg are not so different than the **plight** of the dishwasher in Las Vegas, and that the hopes of the little girl who goes to the **crumbling** school in Dillon are the same as the dreams of the boy who learns on the streets of L. A., we will remember that there is something happening in America, that we are not as divided as our politics suggest, that we are one people, we are one nation. And together we will begin the next great chapter in the American story with three words that will ring from coast to coast, from sea to shining sea: Yes, we can.

21   Thank you New Hampshire. Thank you.

Analysis

The speech "Yes, We Can" is acclaimed as the most inspiring speech of Obama's presidential campaign. He delivered this speech to his supporters after he lost the New Hampshire Democratic Party primary to Hilary Clinton. Despite the loss, he didn't feel discouraged. Instead, he used the opportunity to communicate his political vision and inspire people to fight on. He focused on what they had achieved so far in the face of steep odds, appealing for change and hoping for a better future. The speech served as a rallying call for unity and instilled a sense of hope into his supporters.

This overwhelmingly positive speech is about change, unity, and hope. Obama convinces his followers that change is possible and that Americans, as a unified people, will overcome the obstacles and have a brighter future. In the speech, he addresses the issues people are concerned about, such as health care, a middle-class tax cut, education, the war in Iraq, etc. He makes references to historical events to shape his political vision in a wider context. He uses the three simple words "Yes, We Can" to sum up the spirit of American people and ties it to American dream. He links the three-word creed to some critical moments in American history such as the writing of the Constitution, the abolition of slavery, the expansion of the western frontier, the achievement of women's suffrage, and the first moon landing. It's a patriotic speech in which Obama recalls America's past glories and is looking forward to its bright future passionately. Obama successfully boosts the morale of people and arouses a sense of pride and hope by repeating "Yes, We Can" several times. The three simple words are so strong and powerful that they become

Obama's political slogan to unite people and motivate them to keep on fighting.

Obama uses a variety of rhetorical devices to enhance the impact of the language such as repetition, parallelism, metaphor, alliteration, and so on. The frequent use of parallel structure makes the language very impressive as shown in the following sentences: "There is something happening…" in Paragraphs 3, 4, 5; "there is no problem we cannot solve, there is no destiny…" in Paragraph 6; "We can…" in Paragraph 9; "We will…" in Paragraph 11; "All of the candidates…", "the reason…" in Paragraph 12; "We have been told…, we've been asked,… we've been warned…" in Paragraph 14; "It was…" in Paragraphs 16, 17, 18, 19 and so on. Obama uses the concrete examples in the speech to emphasize the idea that "we are one people", such as specific references to "the textile workers in Spartanburg" and "the dishwasher in Las Vegas". Metaphor is also used ingeniously such as in the sentences "… our climb would be steep" "the battle ahead will be long" and "… lead the nation out of a political darkness". He uses the first person plural frequently, such as "we" or "our" to establish a rapport or bond with people, making them feel united, close, and equal.

The speech is brimming with vigor, passion and inspiration, as well as Obama's superb delivery skills, which appeals to the emotions of the audience. They feel so thrilled and inspired that they chant "Yes, We Can" in response.

Useful Words

abolitionist	n.	废除主义者
ballot	n.	（无记名）投票选举，选票
crumble	v.	（使）破碎，坍塌
cynic	n.	愤世嫉俗者
dissonant	adj.	不和谐的；刺耳的
genocide	n.	种族灭绝，大屠杀
harness	v.	控制；利用
ingenuity	n.	独创力；聪明才智
plight	n.	苦难，困境
tyranny	n.	暴政，专横

Critical Thinking

1. How important is it to tailor a persuasive message to the specific values, attitudes, and beliefs of the audience? What skills can be used to analyze an audience and adapt the message accordingly?

2. Among the four primary methods of persuasion—establishing credibility, supporting ideas with evidence, reasoning, and appealing to emotions—how do they interplay to create a compelling argument?

3. What ethical considerations should a speaker keep in mind to ensure that his or her persuasive efforts are honest and responsible?

4. Why is persuasion considered the most complex and challenging form of public speaking? What additional skills or considerations are required beyond those used in informative speaking?

5. How did the speaker skillfully incorporate emotional appeals in this speech? What can we learn from this technique to effectively engage the emotions of the audience?

7.2 Skill Focus: Speaking to Persuade

7.2.1 Persuasion

According to Lucas, persuasion is the process of creating, reinforcing, or changing people's beliefs or actions. The more you know about persuasion, the more effective you can be in using critical thinking to analyze and assess the large quantity of persuasive information you are exposed to.

When you speak to persuade, you act as an advocator. Your job is to get the audience to agree with you and perhaps to act on that belief. You can use the speaking skills in your speech to inform, and deliver the information clearly and concisely. You should think of your persuasive speech as a kind of mental dialog with your audience, which means you engage in a mental give-and-take with your audience.

Of all kinds of public speaking, persuasion is the most complex and the most challenging. Your objective is more ambitious than in speaking to inform, and the audience analysis and adaptation become much more demanding. The attitudes, values, and beliefs of your audience differ greatly. How successful you are in a persuasive speech will depend on how well you tailor your message to the values, attitudes and beliefs of your audience.

7.2.2 Target Audience

Target audience is the portion of the whole audience that you most want to persuade. As known, you are seldom able to persuade all your audience no matter how hard you try. It only makes sense to decide which portion of the audience you want to reach most.

To properly diagnose the audience, you need to understand who they are. Depending on your topic, you can design a questionnaire to know something about your audience's age, income, ethnicity, race, gender, religion, profession, political affiliation, professional experience, current job title, educational background, etc., which can change the way you frame your topic.

You can use questionnaires to find out where your audience stands on your speech topic. The questionnaire should include questions that indicate how much the audience already knows about the topic, which can help you to determine whether you should focus on the basics, more advanced material, or some points in between. Analyze the audience, take care of their needs and objections, and adapt your message to the values, attitudes and beliefs of the audience, and then you have the chance to deliver a successful persuasive speech.

In most cases, the target audience consist of people who disagree with or are neutral toward your position. You can exclude those from the target audience who are extremely opposed to your position to the point that they probably will not give you a fair hearing. Knowing the target audience's attitudes and gauging how much resistance you're likely to encounter may influence what you say and how you sequence your material. For groups that view your topic negatively, it's generally better to raise their likely objections early in your talk before they raise them for you. Prepare sufficient evidence or material to answer those objections, and then you will have a bigger chance to affect their attitudes, beliefs or actions.

7.2.3 Different Types of Questions

1. Question of Fact

A question of fact is a question about the truth or falsity of an assertion. Propositions or claims of fact are statements with which people disagree and there is evidence on both sides, although probably more on one than on the other. The situation for a persuasive speech on a question of fact is partisan. You act as an advocator with the purpose of presenting one view of the facts as persuasively as possible. You may mention competing views of the facts, but only to refute them.

Examples

(1) Experiments using animals are essential to the development of many life-saving medical procedures.

(2) Climate change is caused by many different human activities.

(3) Watching violence on television causes violent behavior in children.

(4) William Shakespeare did not write most of the plays attributed to him.

2. Question of Value

A question of value is a question about the worth, rightness, morality, and so forth of an idea or action. Such questions not only involve matters of fact, but also demand value judgments. In other words, when the proposition or claim has words such as "good" "bad" "best" "worst" "just" "unjust" "ethical" "unethical" "moral" "immoral" "beneficial" "harmful" "advantageous", or "disadvantageous", it is a question of value.

Examples

(1) Hybrid car is the best form of automobile transportation available today.

(2) In-person schooling is more beneficial for children than online or virtual schooling.

(3) Animal experimentation is (not) ethical.

(4) Chengdu is the most livable city in China.

3. Question of Policy

A question of policy is a question about whether a specific course of action should or should not be taken. These propositions or claims are easy to identify because they almost always have the word "should" in them. They usually fall into two categories: speeches to gain passive agreement and speeches to gain immediate action. If your goal is to gain passive agreement, you will try to convince the audience that a given policy is desirable without encouraging them to take action in support of the policy, while in the second case, you will instigate the audience to action.

Examples for gaining passive agreement

(1) The government should require mandatory recertification of teachers every ten years.

(2) The government should set stricter safety standards for food.

(3) The government should require drivers over the age of 75 to take a vision test and present a certificate of good health from a doctor before renewing their licenses.

Examples for gaining immediate action

(1) Every citizen should start to sort garbage for the sake of environmental protection.

(2) People should act to boycott pirated products.

7.2.4 Organization Based on Types of Persuasive Speeches

1. Organization for a Question of Fact

A persuasive speech on a question of fact is usually organized topically. For example, you want to persuade the audience about the important role of physical exercise in mental well-being. Each main point in your speech can present a reason why the audience should agree with you.

Example

Specific purpose: To persuade your audience that physical exercise can play an important role in mental well-being.

Central idea: There is considerable evidence that physical exercise plays an important role in mental well-being.

Main points:

(1) Exercise decreases stress hormones and increases endorphins—your body's "feel-good" chemicals.

(2) Physical activity distracts you from negative thoughts and emotions.

(3) Exercise decreases sensitivity to the body's reaction to anxiety and even relieves symptoms of mental health conditions like depression and anxiety.

2. Organization for a Question of Value

A persuasive speech on a question of value is usually organized topically. The most common approach is to devote your first main point to establishing the standard of your value judgment, and your second main point to applying those standards to the subject of your speech.

> **Example**
>
> Specific purpose: To persuade the audience that gene editing in human embryos is unethical.
>
> Central idea: Gene editing in human embryos is unethical because it's unsafe, divisive, and unable to ensure justice and equality.
>
> Main points:
>
> 1. Genome-editing research should meet three major ethical standards.
>
> (1) It should be safe.
>
> (2) It should ensure justice and quality.
>
> (3) A broad consensus must be reached by carefully discussing its ethical, legal, and social issues.
>
> 2. Genome-editing research involving embryos can't meet these standards.
>
> (1) Due to the possibility of off-target effects (edits in the wrong place) and mosaicism (when some cells carry the edit but others do not), the premature technique will present safety concerns.
>
> (2) As with many new technologies, genome-editing will only be accessible to the wealthy and will increase existing disparities in access to health care and other interventions.
>
> (3) In many countries, genetically-editing babies has been banned and it is a controversial issue worldwide.

3. Organization for a Question of Policy

Four special patterns are particularly effective for organizing speeches. They are problem-solution order, problem-cause-solution order, comparative advantage order, and motivated sequence.

1) Problem-Solution Order

When you advocate a change in policy, you need to justify it by presenting the needs or reasons. In the first main point, you can demonstrate the need for a new policy by showing the extent and seriousness of the problem. In the second main point, you can explain your plan for solving the problem.

> **Example**
>
> Specific purpose: To persuade your audience to sponsor a child in poverty through a minimal donation.
>
> Central idea: Through a minimal donation each month, you can make the life of a child in the developing world much better.

Main points:

1. Poverty is rampant in many regions of the world and it poses a great threat to children's lives.

(1) 8% of the world's population lives in extreme poverty, according to the World Poverty Clock of the World Data Lab.

(2) Poverty means children do not get adequate health care.

(3) Poverty means children do not get adequate nutrition, and that children are unlikely to reach adult age.

2. Child sponsorship is one of the most effective strategies for addressing poverty.

(1) Through a minimal donation each month, you can help children to get better medical care and reduce the death rate.

(2) Through a minimal donation each month, you can provide essentials like clean water, nutrition, and education for children in poverty.

2) Problem-Cause-Solution Order

This organizational pattern differs slightly from the problem-solution order in which you analyze the causes of the problem. That is, the first main point of the speech should describe a problem, the second analyzes the causes of the problem, and the third recommends a solution to the problem.

Example

Specific purpose: To persuade the audience that American government should enact and implement policies, programs, and practices that reduce easy access to firearms by people.

Central idea: Gun violence is a public health epidemic in the United States that requires action by the government to reduce easy access to firearms by people.

Main points:

1. Gun violence is a public health epidemic in the United States.

(1) Every year nearly 40,000 Americans are killed by guns, including more than 23,000 deaths by firearm suicide and 14,000 deaths by firearm homicide, while the remainder are unintentional of unknown intent or law enforcement intervention.

(2) This equates to more than 100 gun deaths every single day.

2. The cause of gun violence in America is an easy access to firearms.

(1) Many Americans celebrate guns in their culture and disregard the inherent public safety issues that a gun-friendly culture creates.

(2) The U.S. firearm ownership rates exceed those of other high-income countries and Americans own 46% of the world's civilian-owned firearms.

(3) It has been well documented that firearm ownership rates are associated with the increased firearm-related death rates.

3. Gun violence is a complex issue requiring government's efforts on tighter gun control.

(1) Government should enact and implement a true universal background check law that requires background checks on all gun sales and transfers, including private and online sales.

(2) Government should enact and implement policies, programs, and practices that reduce easy access to firearms by people at the risk of interpersonal violence, domestic violence, suicide and mental illness.

3) Comparative Advantage Order

Comparative advantage order is an effective method of organizing a persuasive speech in which each main point explains why a speaker's solution to a problem is preferable to other proposed solutions.

Example

Specific purpose: To persuade the audience that publishing houses should put more emphasis on developing digital books than printed books.

Central idea: Unlike printed books, digital books are environmentally friendly and economical, and can be updated instantly.

Main points:

(1) Unlike printed books, digital books are environmentally friendly.

(2) Unlike printed books, digital books are economical.

(3) Unlike printed books, digital books can be updated instantly to get new editions or information.

4) Motivated Sequence

Motivated sequence is a method of organizing a persuasive speech that seeks immediate action. The five steps of the motivated sequence are attention, need, satisfaction, visualization, and action.

Attention is to capture the attention of the audience by using one of the skills such as telling a story, questioning the audience, beginning with a quotation, startling the audience, relating the topic to the audience, and so on. The second step is need, which means you present the severity of the problem or the compelling situation so as to call for a need to change. Next, you can satisfy the need by providing a solution to the problem. Having given your plan or solution, you visualize what benefits it will bring and what difference it will make. Once the audience is convinced that your policy or plan is beneficial, you instigate the audience to action. In the action step, you can give specific steps for the audience to take as soon as possible to move toward solving the problem.

> **Example**
>
> Specific purpose: To persuade the audience to protect sea animals from water pollution.
>
> Central idea: By reducing water pollution, millions of sea animals can be saved.
>
> Introduction
>
> (Attention: get the attention of the audience)
>
> (1) Do you know there are 5.25 trillion tons of plastic either floating or settled on the sea beds of the oceans worldwide?
>
> (2) Water pollution is leading to the mass extinction of many species of marine life.
>
> (3) In such a compelling situation, you encourage your friend to play a part in protecting sea animals from water pollution.
>
> Body
>
> (Need: make the audience feel a need to change)
>
> 1. Water pollution is affecting marine life in many harmful and threatening ways.
>
> (1) Waste such as metals, plastics, glass, and radioactive drainage is responsible for the killing of hundreds of sea animals each year.
>
> (2) Pollution in general causes global warming, affecting the temperature of oceans threatening marine life.
>
> (3) Water pollution is making the waters around the world hazardous, not only for sea animals but for humans too.
>
> (Satisfaction: satisfy the need by providing a solution to the problem)
>
> 2. You can do whatever you can to save millions of sea animals before it's too late.
>
> (1) You can ban the factories from throwing their wastes in water bodies.
>
> (2) You can reduce the use of plastic and recycle as much as you can.
>
> (3) You can launch "anti-pollution" activities to raise public awareness of protecting the sea and sea animals.
>
> (Visualization: having given your plan, you intensify desire for it by visualizing its benefits)

3. Taking some measures can save millions of sea animals.

(1) Marine life is full of wonders and many new species of underwater organisms.

(2) Saving sea animals is saving human beings.

Conclusion

(Action: call for action)

(1) So I encourage each of you to act and protect sea animals from water pollution.

(2) You will be rewarded with the gift of the nature.

7.2.5 Methods of Persuation

1. Getting Credibility

Credibility is the audience's perception of whether a speaker is qualified to speak on a given topic. Credibility is usually affected by many factors, such as the speaker's sociability, dynamism, physical attractiveness, etc., but above all, it's mainly affected by two factors: competence—how the audience regard the speaker's intelligence, expertise, and knowledge of the subject, and character—how the audience regards the speaker's sincerity, trustworthiness, and concern for the well-being of the audience.

Modern scholars of communication and persuasion speak more about "credibility" as an attitude the audience has towards the speaker, based on both reality and perception, rather than an innate trait of the speaker. Audience members trust the speaker to varying degrees, based on the evidence and knowledge they have about the speaker and how the speaker relates the speech to the values, attitudes and beliefs of the audience.

So how to build and enhance the credibility in a persuasive speech? Here are some tips.

Firstly, explain your competence. In some cases, you are introduced to the audience through the "recommendation" or speech of introduction given by the host. You can build your initial credibility, based on the favorable things the audience already know or believe, such as education, expertise, background, and good character. But if without such a recommendation, you can explain to the audience why you are qualified to speak on the topic and provide your own relevant experience with your topic. Demonstrate that you have done sufficient research on the topic.

> **Example**
>
> I love learning foreign languages. In fact, I love it so much that I like to learn a new language every two years, currently working on my eighth one. When people find that out about me, they always ask me, "How do you do that? What's your secret?" And to be honest, for many years, my answer would be, "I don't know. I simply love learning languages." But people are never satisfied with that answer. They want to know why they are spending years trying to learn even one language, never achieving fluency, and here I come, learning one language after another. They want to know the secret of polyglots, people who speak a lot of languages. And that made me wonder, too, how other polyglots actually do it. What do we have in common? And what is it that enables us to learn languages so much faster than other people? I decided to meet some people like me and find that out. The best place to meet a lot of polyglots is an event where hundreds of language lovers meet in one place to practice their languages. There are several such polyglot events organized all around the world, and so I decided to go there and ask polyglots about the methods that they use. (By Lydia Machova)

Secondly, establish common ground with the audience. Show respect for the audience. Put yourself in your audience's shoes and identify your ideas with those of your audience, trying to show you care about their needs and views.

> **Example**
>
> You're probably familiar with FOMO. That's short for "Fear of Missing Out". It's that feeling you get when it seems everyone else is doing something better than what you're doing now. But there's another FO you need to know about, and it's far more dangerous. It's called FOBO, and it's short for "Fear of a Better Option". We live in a world of overwhelming choice. Even decisions that used to be simple, like choosing a restaurant or making everyday purchases, are now fraught with over analysis. Technology has only made the issue more pronounced. If you want to buy a pair of white shoelaces online, you have to sort through thousands of items and read through hundreds of reviews. That's an astounding amount of information to process to just buy two pieces of string that cost less than your morning latte. Chances are you've experienced FOBO when you've struggled to choose just one from a group of perfectly acceptable outcomes. It's a symptom of a culture which sees value in collecting and preserving as many options as possible. (By Patrick McGinnis)

Thirdly, speak fluently, expressively, and with conviction. The delivery and manners also play important roles in bolstering the credibility. Appear poised and confident, and deliver the speech with genuine conviction. Use the vocal variety to communicate the ideas in a dynamic way. In addition to effective delivery, you should also improve or enhance credibility through citing reliable and authoritative sources and strong arguments and showing awareness of the audience during the speech.

2. Supporting Ideas with Evidence

Evidence is supporting materials used to prove or disprove one thing. If you want to be persuasive, you need to justify your claims by giving evidence. Examples, statistics, and testimony can work as evidence in a persuasive speech.

There are three guidelines for using evidence in a persuasive speech.

(1) Use specific evidence. You state it in specific rather than general terms. Use specific evidence to support your idea, and it will enhance your credibility and make the speech more convincing.

(2) Use novel evidence. You must go beyond what the audience have already known and present new evidence. New evidence is more attention-getting, and you can stand a bigger chance of changing the views of people who disagree with you. In order to be effective, your supporting evidence should be timely and not out of date.

(3) Use evidence from credible sources. If you want to be persuasive, you should use evidence from objective and nonpartisan sources. Citing biased and self-interested sources will diminish the credibility and persuasiveness of the speech.

3. Reasoning

Reasoning is an important part of persuasive speaking. It refers to the process of drawing a conclusion on the basis of evidence. Your speaking is not likely to sway the audience unless your reasoning is clear and logical.

Induction and deduction are the two types of reasoning. Inductive reasoning is probably the form of reasoning you use on a more regular basis. Induction is sometimes referred to as "reasoning from an example or a specific instance to a general conclusion". It can also be called "bottom-up" thinking. In other words, the premises of inductive arguments identify repeated patterns in a sample and general conclusions are inferred for the whole sample. Such conclusions are always considered probable.

> **Examples**
>
> (1) The grouper is a fish which has scales and breathes through its gills.
>
> The sardine is a fish which has scales and breathes through its gills.

The shark is a fish which has scales and breathes through its gills.

Probably all fish have scales and breathes through their gills.

(2) The snake is a reptile and has no hair.

The alligator is a reptile and has no hair.

The tortoise is a reptile and has no hair.

Probably no reptile has hair.

(3) Two times zero equals zero.

Thirty-seven times zero equals zero.

Five hundred and ninety-three times zero equals zero.

So all the numbers multiplied by zero result in zero.

(4) Fish are animals and need oxygen to live.

Mammals are animals and need oxygen to live.

Birds are animals and need oxygen to live.

All animals probably need oxygen to live.

Deduction is a type of reasoning in which a conclusion is based on the combination of multiple premises that are generally assumed to be true. It has been referred to as "reasoning from principle", or a "top-down" reasoning mode. In deductive arguments, the premises from which you start are general principles, from which conclusions about specific cases are inferred. Unlike the inductive arguments, the conclusions of the deductive arguments are always considered valid.

Examples

(1) All mammals have lungs.

　　The dolphin is a mammal.

　　The dolphin has lungs.

(2) The requirement to run for office is to have a Bachelor's degree in Education.

　　Alberto Martínez does not have a degree in Education.

　　Alberto Martínez cannot run for office.

(3) Food with vitamin C supports the immune system.

　　Guava contains vitamin C.

　　Guava supports the immune system.

According to Stephen E. Lucas, there are four basic methods of reasoning—

reasoning from specific instance, reasoning from principle, reasoning from cause, and reasoning from analogy.

1) Reasoning from Specific Instance

Reasoning from specific instance is reasoning that moves from particular facts to a general conclusion. It can also be called generalization, which is a form of inductive reasoning that draws conclusions based on recurring patterns or repeated observations. To generalize, one must observe multiple instances and find common qualities or behaviors and then make a broad or universal statement about them.

When you reason from specific instance, you should follow three basic guidelines. (1) Avoid generalizing too hastily. Your sample of specific instances should be large enough to justify your conclusion. Otherwise, your conclusion is invalid.

Example

Fact 1: The teacher noticed that the 10 students who used the new educational app in her class of 30 showed the significant improvement in their test scores.

Fact 2: In another class, the teacher found that a different group of 10 students using the same app also showed the similar improvement.

Conclusion: The app is universally effective for all students.

The example illustrates a hasty generalization, as the teacher assumes the app's effectiveness across the board without sufficient evidence. A valid conclusion about the app's impact on student performance should be grounded in comprehensive data and a representative sampling of the students.

(2) The instances you give should be fair, unbiased, and representative. Having a large sample size by itself does not guarantee correct conclusions. You need to make sure that the sample you use to make a generalization is representative enough. This is also where the statistical concept of random sampling plays an important role: The respondents should not be too similar, so that your results will be more accurate and representative of the whole people.

(3) Reinforce your argument with statistics or testimony. You can supplement instances with testimony or statistics demonstrating the instances are representative.

Example

Fact 1: 71% of the girls in my school love Science best.

Fact 2: 83% of the boys in my school love Science best.

Conclusion: The students in my school love Science best.

2) Reasoning from Principle

Reasoning from principle is reasoning that moves from a general principle to a specific conclusion. It's a form of deductive reasoning which starts out with a general statement, or hypothesis, and examines the possibilities to reach a specific and logical conclusion. When you use reasoning from principle in a speech, make sure that both the general statement or principle and the minor premise are soundly based.

> **Examples**
>
> (1) Principle: All mammals have backbones. (a general statement)
>
> Minor premise: Humans are mammals. (a minor premise)
>
> Conclusion: Humans have backbones. (a specific conclusion)
>
> (2) Principle: All spiders have eight legs. (a general statement)
>
> Minor premise: A tarantula is a spider. (a minor premise)
>
> Conclusion: Tarantulas have eight legs. (a specific conclusion)

3) Reasoning from Cause

Reasoning from cause is reasoning that seeks to establish the relationship between the cause and effect. It is a form of inductive reasoning you use all the time. There's always a cause-and-effect relationship between two events.

When you use reasoning from cause, beware of the fallacy of false cause. A false cause fallacy occurs when someone incorrectly assumes that a causal relation exists between two things or events. This is an improper conclusion because either such a relationship does not exist or the evidence in support of it is insufficient. A second error to avoid is assuming that events have only one cause. Causes and effects can be very multiple and complicated, so be wary of the temptation to attribute complex events to single causes.

To judge whether the causal reasoning is valid or not, directness and strength make sense. The alleged cause must have a direct relationship with the effect and the cause must be strong enough to produce the effect.

> **Example**
>
> If one person was late for work, he would need to explain the causes. He could suggest the following causes:
>
> (1) His favorite football team lost its game on the night before.
>
> (2) He overslept this morning.

(3) He wore a black shirt which always brought bad luck.

(4) He didn't have a good sleep the night before.

(5) He was stuck in a traffic jam this morning.

Which causes are direct and strong enough to lead to his lateness for work? You can find Number 2 and 5 probably have the most direct effect on his lateness, while the other factors may have slight influence or indirect effect on his emotional or physical state, and Number 3 is considered superstitious. So for Number 2 and 5, the causal reasoning is valid.

4) Reasoning from Analogy

Reasoning from analogy is reasoning in which a speaker compares two similar causes and infers that what is true for the first case is also true for the second. The most important question in assessing analogical reasoning is whether the two cases being compared are essentially alike.

Examples

(1) Humans and laboratory rats are extremely similar biologically, sharing over 90% of their DNA.

(2) Lab rats show promising results when treated with a new drug for managing Parkinson's disease.

Therefore, humans will also show promising results when treated with the drug.

4. Emotional Appeal

Emotional appeal is an important method of persuasion. They're intended to make the audience feel sad, angry, guilty, afraid, happy, proud, sympathetic, reverent, or the like.

You can appeal to these emotions by using emotional language. As is known to all, emotive language pertains to word choice. Specific diction is used to evoke emotion in the audience.

Example

Compare the following sentences:

(1) Put that in the recycle bin. (It is a command but it doesn't cause an emotional reaction.)

(2) You should recycle it because it saves the planet. (This sentence is emotive. It suggests an action and elicits an emotional response.)

(3) Don't you want to save the planet? How could you choose not to recycle since it saves the planet? (Rhetorical question can evoke strong emotions and instigate people to action.)

While delivering a speech, you can use emotive language to attract the attention of the audience, such as the emotive words in the headline. And you can appeal to emotions by developing vivid examples. The use of examples like personal anecdotes or stories is intended to evoke a strong emotional response in the audience, which also makes your words more appealing or convincing. In addition, you should speak with sincerity and conviction. Only in this way is the audience likely to believe, accept what you say, and identify with you.

No matter what kind of emotional appeals you use, remember you need to use it appropriately and ethically. Emotional appeals are appropriate in speeches on questions of policy that seek immediate action from the audience but you should never substitute emotional appeals for evidence and reasoning.

7.2.6 Fallacy

Fallacy is an error in reasoning which can be classified into the following types. You need to think critically and try to avoid fallacious reasoning or logical fallacies when delivering a speech.

1. False Cause

False cause is an error in causal reasoning in which a speaker mistakenly assumes that because one event follows another, and the first event is the cause of the second.

Example

You often hear people complain: "Every time I wash my car, it rains. So it's going to rain because I have washed my car just now." Just because the fact that it rains happens after washing the car, people mistakenly take the first event as the cause of the second. It's a typical false cause fallacy.

2. Invalid Analogy

Invalid analogy is an analogy in which the two cases being compared are not essentially alike in all important aspects.

> **Examples**
>
> (1) Being a teacher is just like being a doctor. Teachers diagnose problems with children and fix them. (These two professions are obviously very different.)
> (2) There's no difference between soccer and tennis. They are both played on a rectangle with balls. (The number of players, balls and game rules are totally different.)

3. Hasty Generalization

Hasty generalization is an error in reasoning from specific instances, in which a speaker jumps to a general conclusion on the basis of insufficient evidence.

> **Examples**
>
> (1) My grandfather has smoked one pack of cigarettes every day for 40 years, but he doesn't have any health problems. So smoking can't be dangerous!
>
> From the example, it can be known that the sample of the specific instance is too small to justify the conclusion, and the generalization is also applied too hastily to other situations.
>
> (2) Premise: Albert Einstein did poorly in math in school.
>
> Conclusion: All world-renowned scientists did poorly in math in school.
>
> Secondary conclusion: I did poorly at math in school, so I will become a world-renowned scientist.

4. Red Herring

Red herring is a fallacy that introduces an irrelevant issue to divert attention from the subject under discussion. It is a misleading statement, a question, or an argument meant to redirect a conversation away from its original topic. It can be found in nearly every kind of communication, whether it be a persuasive essay, an argumentative essay, a debate, a speech, or a conversation. This isn't always for "bad" purposes—sometimes, it's a literary strategy used to keep the audience in suspense.

> **Example**
>
> Person 1: You always leave your stuff all over the room, you don't lock the door behind you, and the trash is piling up. You're a slob!
>
> Person 2: Well, you never pull your car all the way into the driveway, so I'm always stuck having to park on the street!
>
> A person can use a red herring in an argument to distract the other one from the criticism they're making.

5. Ad Hominem

Ad hominem refers to a fallacy that attacks the person rather than dealing with the real issue in dispute. It is a group of argumentation strategies that focus on the person making an argument rather than the viewpoints. This involves an attack on any aspect of the opponent's personality, like his or her intelligence, reputation, or group affiliations. The attack can be subtle, such as casting doubt on a person's character, or overt, like insulting someone.

> **Example 1**
>
> "He is the FIFA World Player of the Year, but don't forget he has been involved in gambling."
>
> The presenter rebuked his personal life rather than commenting on his athletic achievements. The presenter is committing an ad hominem fallacy.

> **Example 2**
>
> Person 1: I think it is important to enforce minimum-wage legislation so that workers are not exploited.
>
> Person 2: Nonsense. You only say that because you just can't get a good job!
>
> Ad hominem fallacy is used as a diversion tactic to shift attention to an unrelated point like a person's character or motive and avoid addressing the actual issue. It is common in both formal and informal contexts, ranging from political debates to online discussions.

6. Bandwagon

Bandwagon is a fallacy that because something is popular, it's good, correct, or desirable. Bandwagon is based on the assumption that the opinion of the majority is always valid, that is, everyone believes it, so you should do it too. It is also called the appeal to popularity, the authority of the many, and the appeal to the people.

> **Example**
>
> Tesla is one of the best-selling electric cars right now. Everyone says it's the best car.
>
> The reasoning behind why the car is the best is that it is popular with people. It's a typical bandwagon fallacy.

Bandwagon is often used as an advertising tactic.

> **Examples**
>
> (1) Carling Lager, Britain's Number One Lager.
> (2) The Steak Escape. America's Favorite Cheesesteak.

7. Slippery Slope

The slippery slope is a fallacy that assumes that taking the first step will lead to subsequent steps that cannot be prevented. The slippery slope fallacy is a logical fallacy that claims one event or action will lead to another more extreme or disastrous event or action. In simple words, if A happens, then B will happen, then C, then D, then E, F, G and it will get worse and worse. Before you know it, all will be in some sort of ruin.

> **Examples**
>
> (1) If students are required to wear uniforms to school, they'll do less shopping at local clothing stores. With less business, the stores will close, which will influence the local economy.
> (2) Widening the road will lead to more traffic in town. More cars on the road will lead to more collisions, which will make the town a dangerous place to drive or walk.

Although it's usually used to argue against taking a specific action, a slippery slope argument isn't, by definition, an argument against something. It's possible to make a slippery slope argument in favor of something.

> **Examples**
>
> (1) By switching to a four-day workweek, employees will have more time to spend with their families. By spending more time with their families, they'll be happier and more productive at work.
> (2) Eliminating tolls will keep more money in tourists' pockets, which they'll spend on local attractions while they're here.

Exercises

I. Decide whether the following statements are TRUE (T), FALSE (F) or NOT GIVEN (NG) according to the Skill Focus in this unit.

1. Persuasion is the process of creating, reinforcing, or changing people's beliefs or actions. (   )

2. In a persuasive speech, the audience engage in a mental give-and-take with the speaker. So the speaker must think of the speech as a mental dialog with the audience. (   )

3. In a persuasive speech, the target audience will consist of people who are neutral toward or slightly in favor of the speaker's position. (   )

4. Persuasive speeches on questions of policy are speeches dealing with questions about the worth, rightness, morality, and so forth of an idea or action. (   )

5. Persuasive speeches on the question of value are always organized in a problem-solution order. (   )

6. When you speak on a question of policy, your goal may be either to gain passive agreement or to motivate immediate action from the audience. (   )

7. The motivated sequence is tailor-made for policy speeches that seek immediate action. It includes five steps: attention, need, satisfaction, visualization, and action. (   )

8. A speaker's credibility has a powerful impact on how well his or her speech is received. One way to boost your credibility is to deliver your speech expressively and with strong eye contact. (   )

II. Choose the best options to answer the following questions or fill in the blanks according to the information given in this unit.

1. _____ is that you progress from a number of particular facts to a general conclusion.
   A. Reasoning from principle
   B. Reasoning from specific instance
   C. Reasoning from cause
   D. Reasoning from analogy

2. Which of the following statements about "using evidence" is NOT true?
   A. Your speech will be more persuasive if you state evidence in specific rather than general terms.
   B. You must go beyond what the audience have already known and present new evidence.
   C. You must use evidence from credible and unbiased sources.
   D. You must rely on the abundant evidence from the Internet.

3. In a speech, you want to persuade an audience about the environmental pollution of takeaway packaging. What kind of speech is it?

A. A persuasive speech on question of fact.
   B. A persuasive speech on question of value.
   C. A persuasive speech on question of policy.
   D. An informative speech about pollution.

4. _____ is a method of organizing persuasive speeches in which each main point explains why a speaker's solution to a problem is preferable to other proposed solutions.
   A. Comparative advantage order   B. Problem-cause-solution order
   C. Topical order   D. Motivated sequence

5. Which of the following statements about "target audience" is TRUE?
   A. You can persuade all your audience if you plot your speech carefully.
   B. In most cases, the target audience will consist of people who are opposed to or neutral towards the speaker's position.
   C. You should concentrate solely on your target audience.
   D. It's meaningless to target at the audience who is strongly opposed, since it's really difficult to convert them.

6. _____ is an error in reasoning in which a speaker mistakenly assumes that because one event follows another, the first event is the cause of the second.
   A. Hasty generalization   B. False cause
   C. Reasoning from analogy   D. Invalid analogy

7. Which of the following is NOT a fallacy?
   A. Generalization.   B. Red herring.
   C. Ad hominem.   D. Bandwagon.

8. _____ assumes that because something is popular, it is good, correct or desirable.
   A. Slippery slope   B. Red herring
   C. Ad hominem   D. Bandwagon

9. When you introduce an irrelevant issue to divert attention from the subject under discussion, you are committing a fallacy: _____.
   A. slippery slope   B. red herring
   C. ad hominem   D. bandwagon

10. Emotional appeals are usually inappropriate in a persuasive speech on _____.
    A. a question of fact   B. a question of value
    C. a question of policy   D. a question of philosophy

7.3 Speaking Task: Making a Persuasive Speech

Task In China, digital payment has almost replaced cash in transactions with the wide use of payment apps such as Alipay and WeChat, while in many other parts of the world, cash payment is still dominant. Which one do you prefer, digital payment or cash? Why do you think so? Conduct a research on this topic and prepare a speech to illustrate the topic with some relevant examples.

7.4 Self-Reflection: Evaluating Your Persuasive Speech

Evaluate your speech based on the rubrics for assessing persuasive speaking. Rate your speech on each point: E—excellent, G—good, A—average, F—fair, P—poor.

Checklist: Persuasive Speech

Items	Scores					Comments
	E	G	A	F	P	
Do you know your target audience quite well?						
Do you introduce the topic clearly?						
Do you establish credibility?						
Do you organize a persuasive speech on a question of fact in topical order?						
Do you devote your first main point to establishing the standards for your value judgment and second main point to applying the standards to the subject in a persuasive speech on a question of value?						

(To be continued)

(Continued)

Items	Scores					Comments
	E	G	A	F	P	
Are your main points in a persuasive speech on a question of policy organized according to one of the following methods of organization? (1) Problem-solution order (2) Problem-cause-solution order (3) Comparative advantage order (4) Motivated sequence						
Are your major points supported by evidence?						
Is your evidence stated in specific, clear terms rather than general ones?						
Do you use evidence that is new to your audience?						
Is your evidence from reliable and unbiased sources?						
Is your reasoning clear and sound?						
Do you reinforce the central idea in the conclusion?						

Unit 8

Using Language Effectively

In this unit you will learn to:

- improve communication skills by mastering the use of language;
- enhance critical thinking and problem-solving abilities through effective language use.

8.1 Speech Reading: I Have a Dream

Activity 1 **Lead-in Listening**

Listen to the speech and summarize it.

Activity 2 **Pre-reading Questions**

1. What is the author's dream as described in the text?

2. How does the repetition of "I have a dream" contribute to the overall tone of the speech?

3. In what ways does the repetition of "I have a dream" serve to engage the audience?

I Have a Dream[1]

1 ... We cannot walk alone.

2 And as we walk, we must make the **pledge** that we shall always march ahead. We cannot turn back. There are those who are asking the devotees of civil rights, "When will you be satisfied?"

3 We can never be satisfied as long as the Negro is the victim of the unspeakable horrors of police **brutality**. We can never be satisfied as long as our bodies, heavy with the fatigue of travel, cannot gain lodging in the motels of the highways and the hotels of the cities. We cannot be satisfied as long as the Negro's basic mobility

---

1 This text is adapted from the Bilibili website.

is from a smaller **ghetto** to a larger one. We can never be satisfied as long as our children are stripped of their self-hood and robbed of their dignity by signs stating: "For Whites Only." We cannot be satisfied as long as a Negro in Mississippi cannot vote and a Negro in New York believes he has nothing for which to vote. No, no, we are not satisfied, and we will not be satisfied until justice rolls down like waters, and righteousness like a mighty stream.

4   I am not unmindful that some of you have come here out of great trials and **tribulations**. Some of you have come fresh from narrow jail cells. And some of you have come from areas where your quest—quest for freedom left you battered by the storms of persecution and **staggered** by the winds of police brutality. You have been the veterans of creative suffering. Continue to work with the faith that unearned suffering is redemptive. Go back to Mississippi, go back to Alabama, go back to South Carolina, go back to Georgia, go back to Louisiana, go back to the slums and ghettos of our northern cities, knowing that somehow this situation can and will be changed. Let us not wallow in the valley of despair.

5   I say to you today, my friends, so even though we face the difficulties of today and tomorrow, I still have a dream. It is a dream deeply rooted in the American dream.

6   I have a dream that one day this nation will rise up and live out the true meaning of its **creed**: "We hold these truths to be self-evident; that all men are created equal."

7   I have a dream that one day on the red hills of Georgia, the sons of former slaves and the sons of former slave owners will be able to sit down together at the table of brotherhood.

8   I have a dream that one day even the state of Mississippi, a state **sweltering** with the heat of injustice, sweltering with the heat of oppression, will be transformed into an **oasis** of freedom and justice.

9   I have a dream that my four little children will one day live in a nation where they will not be judged by the color of their skin but by the content of their character.

10   I have a dream today!

11   I have a dream that one day, down in Alabama, with its vicious racists, with its governor having his lips **dripping with** the words of "**interposition**" and "**nullification**", that one day right down in Alabama little black boys and black girls will be able to join hands with little white boys and white girls as sisters and brothers.

12   I have a dream today!

13   I have a dream that one day every valley shall be **exalted**, and every hill and mountain shall be made low, the rough places will be made plain, and the crooked places will be made straight; "and the glory of the Lord shall be revealed and all flesh shall see it together."

14   This is our hope. This is the faith that I go back to the South with. With this faith, we will be able to hew out of the mountain of despair a stone of hope. With this faith, we will be able to transform the **jangling** discords of our nation into a beautiful symphony of brotherhood. With this faith, we will be able to work together, to pray together, to struggle together, to go to jail together, to stand up for freedom together, knowing that we will be free one day.

15   This will be the day when all of God's children will be able to sing with new meaning, "My country, 'Tis of Thee①, sweet land of liberty, of thee I sing. Land where my fathers died, land of the Pilgrim's pride, from every mountainside, let freedom ring!"

16   And if America is to be a great nation, this must become true. So let freedom ring from the **prodigious** hilltops of New Hampshire. Let freedom ring from the mighty mountains of New York. Let freedom ring from the heightening Alleghenies of Pennsylvania. Let freedom ring from the snow-capped Rockies of Colorado. Let freedom ring from the **curvaceous** slopes of California. But not only that; let freedom ring from the stone Mountain of Georgia. Let freedom ring from Lookout Mountain Tennessee. Let freedom ring from every hill and molehill of Mississippi. From every mountainside, let freedom ring.

...

Analysis

The text is an excerpt from Martin Luther King Jr.'s famous speech—"I Have a Dream" delivered during March on Washington for Jobs and Freedom in 1963. In the speech, King addresses the struggles and injustices faced by African Americans in the United States and emphasizes the need for civil rights and racial equality. He expresses the dissatisfaction with the current state of affairs and outlines his dream for a future where all individuals are judged by their character rather than their skin color. King envisions a nation where racial segregation and discrimination are eradicated, and people of all backgrounds can come together in unity. He calls for freedom, justice, and equality to "ring" across the nation, using powerful imagery and references to various geographical locations.

The argument in the speech is effectively presented through the use of supporting evidence, emotional appeal, and vivid imagery. King provides examples of the injustices faced by African Americans, such as police brutality, segregation, and voter disenfranchisement. These examples serve as concrete evidence of the need for change and support his call for racial equality. The emotional appeal in his words connects deeply with the audience's emotions, invoking empathy and understanding for the struggles experienced by African Americans.

King's use of vivid imagery creates a sense of unity and aspiration. By referencing various states and geographical features, he symbolically extends his message to encompass the entire nation, emphasizing that the struggle for civil rights is not isolated to one region. This use of imagery helps to unify the audience and emphasizes the universality of his message.

The speech's repetition of the phrase "I have a dream" serves as a rhetorical device that reinforces King's vision for a better future. This repetition not only emphasizes the central theme of the speech but also makes the argument memorable and impactful. Overall, the article effectively presents its argument by employing compelling examples, emotional appeal, vivid imagery, and rhetorical techniques that resonate with the audience and communicate a powerful message of hope, unity, and equality.

Useful Words & Expression

brutality	n.	残酷，残忍行径
creed	n.	信条，信念；教义
curvaceous	adj.	（女子）曲线优美的，身材匀称丰满的
exalt	v.	晋升，提拔
ghetto	n.	（尤指城市中贫穷的）某种族（或宗教信仰者）聚居区；贫民区
interposition	n.	插入；介入
jangling	n.	丁零当啷声
nullification	n.	无效，废弃，取消；（美）州对联邦法令的拒绝执行或承认
oasis	n.	（繁忙、令人不适环境之中的）宁静宜人之地
pledge	n.	誓言，诺言，保证
prodigious	adj.	强大的，巨大的
stagger	v.	使震惊，使大吃一惊
swelter	v.	（人）感觉热极了
tribulation	n.	苦难，艰难
dripping with		充满

Note

My Country, 'Tis of Thee: It refers to the lyrics of "My Country" and "Tis of Thee" is also known as "America". The words were written by Samuel Francis Smith in 1831 when he was a student. The song was first publicly performed on July 4, 1831, at a National Day celebration in Boston and served as the national anthem of the United States during the 19th century.

Critical Thinking

1. How does using concrete language enhance the audience's understanding of abstract concepts? What are the potential pitfalls of being overly abstract in speech?

2. What is the role of precision in ensuring that the audience accurately interprets the speaker's message? How can a speaker avoid ambiguity while still engaging the audience?

3. How can the use of inclusive language help to build rapport with a diverse audience? What strategies can a speaker employ to ensure his or her language is inclusive and respectful of all audience members?

4. How does the use of familiar language or references help to connect with the audience? Can overusing familiar language or references potentially alienate certain audience members?

5. In "I Have a Dream", how did the use of rhetorical devices, such as parallelism and metaphors, effectively convey the message of racial equality and justice while maintaining the ethical integrity of the speech?

8.2 Skill Focus: Using Language Effectively

Language is an important aspect of speech. From the actual words to the points and themes that you articulate, language is a tool that helps your audience to understand and agree with what you are saying or making.

8.2.1 Being Concrete

Being concrete means that you should provide clearer information using specific words instead of general words in your speech. Instead of using general words like "everything" "very" or "a lot", you can replace them with a more specific term. Here are two strategies that can help you to use specific language.

The first one is to replace abstract terms using concrete words with clear and direct meanings.

> **Example**
>
> Abstract: The case sought to establish equality for people of all sexual orientations.
> Analysis: Equality can mean a variety of things to different people. What does equality mean in this example?
> Concrete: Inheritance treats individuals and couples of all sexual orientations equally.

The second one is to make use of language that engages the senses.

> **Example**
>
> Abstract: The waiting room was unpleasant.
> Analysis: What makes this setting unpleasant? Replace the term with specific and descriptive words.
> Concrete: The waiting room was cold, antiseptic-smelling, and crowded with sick people who were coughing, groaning, or crying.

8.2.2 Being Precise

The list of ambiguous terms and phrases that have been clarified is as follows. In your speech, you should try to use more precise words to make your speech easily understood.

The List of Ambiguous Terms and Phrases

Vague	Precise
many, a lot	ten, sixteen, one thousand, etc.
cool (referring to temperature)	50 degrees Fahrenheit, 35 degrees Celsius, etc.
most	90%, 94%, etc.
later / very soon	4:00 p.m., 10:00 p.m. / in ten minutes / tomorrow morning at 8:00, etc.
staff	supervisors, accountants, nurse practitioners, etc.

8.2.3 Being Inclusive

Being inclusive in the delivery of speech is crucial for creating a diverse and respectful society. Language has the power to either engage or alienate the audience, and using language that isn't inclusive can quickly turn off a crowd. It is essential to avoid placing any group of people above or below other groups when speaking about gender, race, or impairments.

One common area of contention when it comes to language that refers to gender is the use of gender-specific pronouns. Instead of relying on traditional terms like "he" or "she", individuals should be referred to by their chosen name, title, or gender-neutral pronouns. This not only eliminates confusion but also promotes inclusivity and respect for individuals regardless of their gender.

Similarly, when referring to individuals based on their race or ethnicity, it is important to avoid using stereotype and offensive language. Stereotype can perpetuate harmful biases and contribute to a lack of understanding between different racial or ethnic groups.

As for discussing impairments, it is essential to use language that is inclusive and respectful of individuals with disabilities. Language plays a crucial role in how people with disabilities are perceived and treated by others. One common issue related to disability is the use of derogatory language or stereotypes, which can perpetuate harmful biases and contribute to a lack of understanding between people with disabilities and those without. Terms like "cripple" or "retard" are outdated and offensive and should be avoided instead of using more inclusive language such as "person with a disability" or "person with a mobility challenge". By avoiding these types of language, you can create a more respectful and supportive environment for people with disabilities during the speech. Additionally, it is important to ensure that public spaces and accommodations are accessible to individuals with disabilities, rather than relying on assumptions or stereotypes about their needs.

In addition, you can increase your chances of getting the audience convince that your subject matter is serious and vital to them by utilizing language that clearly relates your topic or argument to the audience. It can be subtle to persuade your audience to pay attention by using words like "us" "you" and "we". Make these connections evident for the audience by utilizing language that is specific to them because most people are interested in the topics that have a direct impact on their lives.

8.2.4 Being Familiar

Being familiar with the language you use is crucial for the success of a speech. Using an unfamiliar language can make it difficult to speak honestly, and ultimately it will affect the trust with the audience and how your speech is received by the audience. It is important to ensure that the language you use is both familiar to you and the audience.

One aspect of being familiar with the language you use is understanding its nuances and idiomatic expressions. Certain words or phrases may have different meanings depending on the context in which they are used. Understanding these nuances can help you to avoid confusion or misunderstandings when delivering a speech.

Another aspect of being familiar with the language you use is knowing your audience. Different groups of people may have different levels of familiarity with certain terms or expressions. Being familiar with the language you use also involves using appropriate vocabulary and grammar. Using overly complex or technical terms can make your speech difficult to follow and understand. Similarly, using incorrect grammar or sentence structures can lead to confusion and undermine the credibility of your message.

8.2.5 Being Rhetorical

Rhetoric is a crucial aspect of effective speechmaking. It refers to the art of using language effectively and persuasively to convey meaning and influence others. When you uses rhetorical devices, you are able to capture the attention of the audience, create an emotional connection, and communicate the message effectively.

One of the most important roles of rhetoric in speechmaking is the ability to persuade the audience. When delivering a speech, you should learn to appeal to the audience's emotions, logic, and ethics. By appealing to these different aspects of the audience's psyche, you can more effectively convince them of your point of view.

Another key role of rhetoric in speeches is to create a memorable and impactful message. A powerful speech often incorporates metaphor, and other rhetorical devices that stick in the minds of the audience long after the speech has ended. This can help to reinforce the message and make it more likely to be remembered by the audience.

In addition to its practical benefits, rhetoric can also add depth and nuance to your message. By using carefully chosen words and phrases, you can convey complex ideas in a way that is both engaging and easy to understand. This can help to ensure that the audience can fully understand the message being presented.

To make a successful delivery of speech, the following rhetorical devices can be used.

1) Metaphor and Simile

The audience will be able to conjure up powerful, distinctive, memorable images thanks to vivid language. The audience are more likely to fully comprehend and picture what you are saying when you use good vivid language.

Metaphor is the rhetorical device that is made between two things. Simile function similarly as metaphor. Metaphor does not use the comparison-making words "like" or "as", but simile does. The strength of a metaphor lies in its capacity to imbue the viewer with an emotional image. Simile makes the message clearer by using ideas that are more specific to your audience, which is used to convey a clearer and more vivid message.

2) Alliteration

Alliteration is the repetition of the initial sounds of words which is a useful tool to help the audience to remember your message. It's as simple as taking a few moments to see whether there are ways to change the language so you can add alliteration, especially when it comes to the things you want the audience to remember the most.

3) Antithesis

Antithesis allows you to use contradictory statements to make a rhetorical point. This technique of presenting opposing ideas side by side is often used to make a compelling argument and grab the audience's attention.

4) Parallelism

Parallel structure is the balance of two or more similar clauses or sentences, while parallel phrasing is the balance of two or more similar words. When delivering a speech, it is important to be mindful of your wording and delivery in order to convey your message effectively. By using creative and tense language, as well as incorporating pauses, you can make your speech more dramatic and memorable. Additionally, utilizing parallel language and structure can help you to speak persuasively. By employing these strategies, you can create a speech that flows naturally and leads the audience to your desired conclusion.

5) Repetition

Speech is delivered orally, so the audience need to get the core of the message repeated throughout. Repetition aims to help the audience to become familiar with the short sections of the speech by listening to them once more.

Exercises

Answer the following questions according to the Skill Focus in this unit.

1. What does the author say is an important aspect of speech?
2. What should speakers do to use specific language?
3. What is a gender-specific pronoun used for?
4. How can speakers increase the chances of getting their audience to listen and be convinced?
5. How can speakers pique their audience's interest in their subject or inspire them to care about their point of view?
6. What is the purpose of being familiar with language?

8.3 Speaking Task: Delivering the Opening Address at a Conference

Task Choose either of the one-paragraph examples and deliver the opening address at a conference.

Example 1

Ladies and Gentlemen, Esteemed Colleagues, and Distinguished Guests,

It is with immense pride that I welcome you to the International Conference on Sustainable Development. Imagine a tapestry of our collective dreams, woven with threads of hope and determination. Today, we stand at the loom, ready to weave a future that is not only prosperous but also in rhythm with the heartbeat of our planet. As we gather under this shared sky, we carry with ourselves the dreams of generations past and the aspirations of those yet to come. Over the next few days, this conference will be our stage, where we will engage in dialogues that challenge the status quo, explore solutions that are as innovative as they are necessary, and foster collaborations that are the lifeblood of progress. We will embark on a journey of discovery, where each conversation is a step towards a more sustainable world.

Example 2

Ladies and Gentlemen, Esteemed Colleagues, and Distinguished Guests,

> As we convene for the International Conference on Sustainable Development, I am deeply honored to extend to you a warm welcome. Let us begin with a thought that has echoed through the ages, a quote by the renowned environmentalist and author, Rachel Carson: "In nature, nothing exists alone." As we gather here today, we are not just individuals; we are part of a larger ecosystem of ideas, dreams, and aspirations. In the words of another visionary, Mahatma Gandhi, "Be the change you wish to see in the world." Let us embody this call for action as we navigate the corridors of this conference, each step forward a testament to our shared resolve to shape a more sustainable world.
>
> **Example 3**
>
> Ladies and Gentlemen, Esteemed Colleagues, and Distinguished Guests,
>
> It is my great honor to welcome you to the International Conference on Sustainable Development. As we gather here today, we do not just carry the collective hope of shaping a future that is prosperous and in harmony with our planet. We also carry the weight of startling data that demands our urgent attention. Did you know that if current consumption patterns continue, we would need the resources of three Earths to sustain our needs by 2050? This alarming statistic should serve as a clarion call to action, underscoring the urgency of our mission. Over the next few days, we will not only engage in thought-provoking discussions but also confront the hard truths revealed by data that can no longer be ignored.

8.4 Self-Reflection: Evaluating Your Opening Address

Evaluate your speech based on the information in the following table. Rate your speech on each point: E—excellent, G—good, A—average, F—fair, P—poor.

Checklist: Opening Address

Items	Scores					Comments
	E	G	A	F	P	
Opening Was the opening stimulating and powerful? Did it capture the audience's attention? Did it have impact?						

(To be continued)

(Continued)

Items	Scores					Comments
	E	G	A	F	P	
Manner Direct, confident, authentic, calm, professional, lively, bold, powerful, gentle, caring?						
Content Was there a logical beginning, middle and end? Did you use stories, anecdotes or metaphors to illustrate points?						
Body language Natural and relaxed gestures, good posture, Confident and expressive expressions?						
Facial expression Smiling, expressive, open, no twitching?						
Eye contact Alive, energetic, looking at the audience?						
Vocal quality Varied pitch, pauses, good pace, passionate?						
Volume Easy to hear? Projection?						
Language Is it appropriate for the audience?						
Group participation Did the audience get involved? Any questions?						
Tone Energetic and enthusiastic? Passionate or boring?						
Ending Powerful, memorable, challenging, finishing with a bang?						

Unit 9

Supporting Your Ideas

In this unit you will learn to:

- explain why supporting materials are necessary;
- get to know the various types of verbal supporting materials;
- discuss supporting material strengths in explaining and proving ideas and arguments;
- incorporate supporting materials seamlessly into the speech;
- use supporting materials ethically through correct citation.

9.1 Speech Reading: We Shall Fight on the Beaches

Activity 1 Lead-in Listening

Listen to the speech and complete the table.

Topic	Description	Examples	Key Takeaway
Man and desire		1. Men have instinctual responses like hunger and warmth. 2. Desire requires forces beyond ourselves. 3. Thick desires are shaped by models of parents and admired individuals. 4. Thin desires are highly mimetic and ephemeral. 5. Identifying thin and thick desires is key to taking control over our lives.	1. Embrace thick desires rooted in core human truths. 2. Be aware of thin desires that can change rapidly. 3. Take time for recollection and self-discovery. 4. Listen to life and understand how relationships and desires grow.

(To be continued)

(Continued)

Topic	Description	Examples	Key Takeaway
Mimesis in desire	Desire is imitative, as we look to models of what to want.	1. _____ 2. _____	1. Seek models that align with core human values. 2. Be open to new desires as models change. 3. Reflect on the role of mimesis in shaping your desires.
	There are two kinds of desire: thick desires shaped by models over time and thin desires that are easily shifted by external factors.	1. Career changes due to thin desires without rooting in thick desires. 2. Thin desires like leaves blown away by wind. 3. Recognizing the difference between thick and thin desires is crucial for fulfillment.	1. Cultivate thick desires based on core values. 2. Allow for flexibility in thin desires but not at the cost of your sense of purpose. 3. Stay grounded in your journey by reflecting on your past fulfillment stories.
Listening for transformation	To transform our desires, we need to listen to our lives and understand our true selves.	1. Parker Palmer's quote about listening to life before making decisions. 2. The importance of identifying personal fulfillment stories. 3. The role of reflection in understanding our relationships and desires.	1. _____ 2. _____ 3. _____

Activity 2 Pre-reading Questions

1. Why is it important to never give up, even when facing challenges or setbacks?

2. What are some strategies that can help people to stay motivated and persevere in the face of adversity?

149

3. Can you share some inspiring stories or examples of people who refused to give up and achieved great success despite facing difficulties?

We Shall Fight on the Beaches[1]

...

1   When we consider how much greater would be our advantage in defending the air above this Island against an overseas attack, I must say that I find in these facts a sure basis upon which practical and reassuring thoughts may rest. I will pay my **tribute** to these young airmen. The great French Army was very largely, for the time being, **cast back** and disturbed by the **onrush** of a few thousands of armored vehicles. May it not also be that the cause of civilization itself will be defended by the skill and devotion of a few thousand airmen? There never has been, I suppose, in all the world, in all the history of war, such an opportunity for youth. The Knights of the Round Table, the Crusaders,① all **fall back** into the past not only distant but **prosaic**; these young men, going forth every morn to guard their native land and all that we stand for, holding in their hands these instruments of **colossal** and **shattering** power, of whom it may be said that.

2   Every morn brought forth a noble chance. And every chance brought forth a noble knight, deserve our gratitude, as do all the brave men who, in so many ways and on so many occasions, are ready, and continue ready to give life and all for their native land.

3   I return to the Army. In the long series of very fierce battles, now on this front, now on that, fighting on three fronts at once, battles fought by two or three divisions against an equal or somewhat larger number of the enemy, and fought fiercely on some of the old grounds that so many of us knew so well-in these battles our losses in men have exceeded 30,000 killed, wounded and missing. I take occasion to express the sympathy of the House② to all who have suffered bereavement or who are still anxious. The President of the Board of Trade [Sir Andrew Duncan] is not here today. His son has been killed, and many in the House have felt the pangs of affliction in the sharpest form. But I will say this about the missing. We have had a large number of wounded come home safely to this country, but I would say about the missing that there may be very many reported missing who will come back home, some day, in one way or another. In the confusion of this fight it is inevitable that many have been left in positions where honor required no further resistance from them.

---

1 This text is adapted from the Winstonchurchill website.

4   Against this loss of over 30,000 men, we can set a far heavier loss certainly inflicted upon the enemy. But our losses in material are enormous. We have perhaps lost one-third of the men we lost in the opening days of the battle of 21st March, 1918, but we have lost nearly as many guns—nearly one thousand and all our transport, all the armored vehicles that were with the Army in the north. This loss will impose a further delay on the expansion of our military strength. That expansion had not been proceeding as far as we had hoped. The best of all we had to give had gone to the British Expeditionary Force[③], and although they had not the numbers of tanks and some articles of equipment which were desirable, they were a very well and finely equipped Army. They had the first-fruits of all that our industry had to give, and that is gone. And now here is this further delay. How long it will be and how long it will last depend upon the exertions which we make in this Island. An effort the like of which has never been seen in our records is now being made. Work is proceeding everywhere, night and day, Sundays and week days. Capital and Labor have **cast aside** their interests, rights, and customs and put them into the common stock. Already the flow of munitions has leaped forward. There is no reason why we should not in a few months **overtake** the sudden and serious loss that has come upon us, without **retarding** the development of our general program.

5   Nevertheless, our thankfulness at the escape of our Army and so many men, whose loved ones have passed through an **agonizing** week, must not blind us to the fact that what has happened in France and Belgium is a colossal military disaster. The French Army has been weakened, the Belgian Army has been lost, a large part of those fortified lines upon which so much faith had been reposed is gone, many valuable mining districts and factories have passed into the enemy's possession, the whole of the Channel[④] ports are in his hands, with all the tragic consequences that follow from that, and we must expect another blow to be struck almost immediately at us or at France. We are told that Herr Hitler has a plan for invading the British Isles. This has often been thought of before. When Napoleon lay at Boulogne for a year with his flat-bottomed boats and his Grand Army, he was told by someone. "There are bitter weeds in England." There are certainly a great many more of them since the British Expeditionary Force returned.

...

> ### Analysis
>
> The speech discusses the current situation of Britain during World War II. The presenter emphasizes the importance of defending the airspace above the island against overseas attacks, drawing parallels between the young airmen of the Royal Air Force and historical figures like the Knights of the Round Table and the Crusaders. The presenter

praises the dedication and skill of these airmen who defend the nation.

The speech also reflects on recent military losses, both in terms of personnel and material. While British losses in men have exceeded 30,000 in fierce battles, the enemy has also suffered heavy losses. Besides, the British forces have lost a significant number of guns, vehicles, and equipment, which will impact their military strength. The presenter acknowledges the sympathy for those who have suffered losses, particularly mentioning the son of a government official who was killed in action.

The presenter discusses the need for a strong defense against potential invasion, especially with the threat of the enemy's possession of Channel ports. The focus is on organizing defenses within the island to ensure security and potential offensive capabilities. The speech suggests that a secret session of the House might be appropriate to discuss defense strategies without revealing military secrets to the enemy.

Overall, the speech's arguments are centered around the need for strong defense, the sacrifices made by the military personnel, the challenges posed by losses, and the necessity of preparing for potential invasion.

The speech makes a good argument by presenting a clear and coherent narrative that emphasizes the importance of defense, acknowledges the sacrifices of the military, and addresses challenges related to losses and potential threats. It uses historical references to evoke a sense of duty and highlights the current efforts being made to strengthen the defense of the Island. Additionally, the presenter's willingness to consider a secret session for discussing defense strategies demonstrates a prudent approach to balancing the transparency with security.

Useful Words & Expressions

agonizing	adj.	苦恼的；痛苦难忍的
colossal	adj.	巨大的，庞大的
onrush	n.	猛然而来，突如其来
overtake	v.	超过，赶上
prosaic	adj.	乏味的，无聊的
retard	v.	阻碍，减缓
shattering	adj.	令人震惊的，令人极度悲痛的
tribute	n.	致敬
cast back		退回
cast aside		消除，废除
fall back		后退

Notes

① the Crusaders: They are Catholic soldiers, who participated in the Crusades, wearing the symbol of the cross.

② the House: The Parliament is the central part of British politics and the supreme legislative body of the United Kingdom. The Prime Minister emerges from Parliament and is accountable to it. The U.K. Parliament is bicameral, consisting of the House of Lords and the House of Commons.

③ The British Expeditionary Force (BEF): It refers to the military units that the U.K. dispatched to the European mainland to fight during both World Wars. During World War I, the British sent the BEF to assist France in combat against the German forces, participating in battles such as the Battle of the Marne, the Battle of Ypres, and the Battle of Cambrai. In World War II, the British dispatched the BEF to assist France against Germany, but later evacuated their forces twice in response to the German advance.

④ the Channel: It is also known as the Strait of Dover, which is the strait that separates the UK from the European mainland and connects the Atlantic Ocean with the North Sea. The channel is 560 kilometers (350 miles) long, and at its narrowest point, known as the Strait of Dover, it is only 34 kilometers (21 miles) wide. Dover in the United Kingdom and Calais in France face each other across the strait.

Critical Thinking

1. How can a speaker seamlessly incorporate supporting materials into his or her speech without disrupting the flow of the presentation? What skills can be used to ensure that supporting materials are introduced and explained clearly?

2. Why is it important to use supporting materials ethically by citing sources correctly? How can a speaker ensure he or she is giving proper credit to the original creators of the supporting materials?

3. How do supporting materials, such as visual aids and interactive elements, help maintain audience attention and engagement throughout a presentation? What strategies can be used to capture and sustain the audience's interest?

4. How can exploring different types of supporting materials enhance a speaker's ability to convey complex ideas? What are some creative ways to incorporate a variety of supporting materials into a presentation?

5. In "We Shall Fight on the Beaches", how did the speaker use specific historical events and the imminent threat of invasion to bolster his speech with compelling and persuasive supporting materials?

9.2 Skill Focus: Supporting Your Ideas

Supporting materials are essential to a successful presentation as it helps to reinforce and clarify the main points of your presentation. By providing additional information, examples, and context, supporting material makes your message more persuasive and engaging for the audience. Supporting material can help to explain and prove ideas and arguments. It provides additional evidence or examples that can help to strengthen your main points and make them more convincing. Additionally, it helps to fill in the gaps in your argument and provides the context which is difficult to achieve through direct speech alone.

To incorporate supporting materials seamlessly into your speech, you should practice delivering them effectively. This means practicing how you will introduce and explain each piece of supporting materials, and making sure that you deliver it with clarity and confidence. Additionally, it's important to use supporting materials ethically by citing your sources correctly and giving credit where it is due.

In this unit, what supporting materials are, what they do, and how to use them effectively will be discussed. You will also explore some examples of different types of supporting materials that can be used in your presentation.

9.2.1 Supporting Materials

Supporting materials including visual aids such as slide, chart, and graph, as well as verbal aids such as note, summary, and restatement serve several important functions in a presentation. (1) They help to reinforce your main points by providing additional information and examples that support your argument. This makes your message more persuasive and helps to keep your audience engaged throughout the presentation. (2) Supporting materials provide context and background information that can help your audience to better understand the significance of your main points. By providing relevant facts, statistics, and case studies, you can help your audience to see the relevance of your message to their own lives or work. (3) Supporting materials can help to break up the monotony of a long presentation by offering variety and interest. By using different types of supporting materials such as visual aids, verbal aids, and interactive elements, you can keep your audience engaged and interested throughout the presentation.

Using supporting materials effectively is key to ensuring that they enhance your message rather than detract from it. Here are some tips for using supporting materials effectively.

(1) Be selective. It's important to choose supporting materials that are relevant and add value to your message. Don't just include something that comes to your mind. Instead, consider which piece of information will be most helpful to your audience.

(2) Keep it simple. While it's important to include supporting materials in your presentation, it's equally important not to overwhelm your audience with too much information. Choose one or two key pieces of supporting materials throughout the presentation, and focus on delivering them clearly and concisely.

(3) Use visual aids sparingly. Visual aids such as slide can be effective when used correctly, but it can also be distracting if it is overused or poorly designed. Use visual aids only when they directly support your main points and help to illustrate complex ideas.

(4) Practice more. Practice makes perfect. Practice more before your presentation to make sure that you can deliver the speech effectively.

9.2.2 Types of Supporting Materials

In the art of the effective delivery of speech, the choice of supporting materials can be the key to delivering a compelling message. There are eight diverse types of supporting materials at your disposal: examples, narratives, definitions, description, historical and scientific facts, statistics, testimonies, and quotations. Each of these types offers a unique approach to reinforcing your message, catering to different purposes, and engaging the varied audience. Understanding when and how to deploy these supporting materials are essential for crafting persuasive arguments, captivating stories, or informative presentations.

1. Examples

Examples are supporting materials that can be used to clarify and reinforce the main points of your presentation. They provide concrete, specific instances that help to illustrate and emphasize your message. However, it's important to keep in mind that examples are most effective when they are tailored to your audience's experiences and knowledge.

To use examples effectively, it's important to choose those that are relevant and relatable to your audience. Avoid using overly general or abstract examples that may not resonate with the audience. Instead, look for examples that people can easily relate to or that highlight the key concepts you want to convey.

In addition to being clear and relevant, examples should also be well-chosen and well-presented. Make sure that your examples are vivid and descriptive, helping your audience to visualize them and better understand the concept you are trying to illustrate.

2. Narratives

Narratives including stories and anecdotes are a powerful tool for speakers to engage their audience and convey their message. It can be used effectively in the introduction, body, and conclusion of a speech to interest the audience, clarify ideas, dramatize concepts, and emphasize key points. When done well, narrative has strong emotional power that can help to connect with the audience and leave a lasting impression.

One of the benefits of using narratives in your speech is that it can help to capture the audience's attention right from the start. A well-crafted story or anecdote can pique the audience's curiosity. Additionally, narrative can help to break up the monotony of a long presentation by providing a change of pace and adding variety.

In terms of content, narratives can come in many different forms. Personal narratives are particularly effective because they are relatable and speak directly to the audience's experiences. Literary narratives can also be powerful, as they often draw on universal themes and emotions that resonate with people across cultures and time periods. Historical narratives can provide context and help to illustrate complex ideas by relating them to real-world events. Hypothetical narratives, such as thought experiments or case studies, can be used to explore new ideas and challenge assumptions.

When crafting narratives for your speech, it's important to keep in mind the purpose of the narrative and how they fit into your overall message. Narratives should be relevant and support your main points, rather than distract from them. Additionally, they should be well-structured and easy to follow with a clear beginning, middle, and end.

By choosing relevant and well-crafted stories and anecdotes, you can help the audience to better understand complex ideas and concepts, making your presentation more engaging and persuasive.

3. Definitions

Defining words is important to the delivery of speech, particularly in specialized topics about medicine, law, technology, and art. By setting limits on the meanings and interpretations of words, you should ensure that the audience can understand the content of the speech correctly.

There are two main types of definitions: denotative and connotative. Denotative definition provides a straightforward explanation of the word's meaning based on its dictionary definition. Connotative definition provides a deeper understanding of the word's meaning by exploring its cultural or emotional associations.

It's important to note that not all words have clear-cut denotative or connotative definitions. Some words may have multiple meanings or interpretations that depend on context or cultural background. In these cases, it's up to you to provide guidance on how the word should be understood.

One effective way to define unfamiliar or complex words is to use stipulated definitions early in the speech. This involves providing a clear and objective definition of the term before diving into the main topic of the speech. Stipulated definitions can be particularly useful for terms that have confusing or controversial meanings, as they help to establish common ground and ensure that everyone is on the same page.

Another approach to defining words is to use synonyms or related terms to provide additional context and clarification. Synonyms can be helpful when defining technical terms or jargon that may be unfamiliar to the audience. However, it's important to choose synonyms that accurately convey the intended meaning and avoid using vague or misleading ones.

In addition to using defined terms, it's also important to be mindful of how words are used in context. The same word may have different meanings depending on the situation or the audience, so speakers should strive to use language that is clear, concise, and appropriate for their message.

4. Descriptions

Description is a powerful tool that can help to make your speech more engaging and memorable. By using the five senses—sight, hearing, taste, smell, and touch—you can create vivid and immersive descriptions that allow your audience to experience what you're talking about. Additionally, by incorporating kinesthetic (movement of the body) and organic (internal physical feeling) descriptions, you can provide a more comprehensive understanding of the topic at hand.

To use description effectively as supporting material, it's important to think in terms of the five questions of what, where, how, who, and when. By answering these questions in detail, you can provide context and background information that can help the audience to understand the topic more deeply. It's also important to be specific and concrete in your speech, using concrete examples whenever possible.

Describing processes is also another useful way to support your message with description. This approach is particularly useful when discussing complex topics or processes that may be unfamiliar to the audience. To effectively describe a process, you need to provide enough detail to allow the audience to follow along without getting lost or confused. This often requires going beyond just the basic steps involved in the process and providing explanations of why certain steps are necessary or how they contribute to the overall outcome.

5. Historical and Scientific Facts

Using historical and scientific facts as supporting materials in your speech can be an effective way to provide evidence for your argument and help to clarify your points. It's important to use these facts wisely and accurately, ensuring that you are citing reliable sources.

One key consideration when using historical or scientific facts is to make sure that they are actually true. This means doing your research and checking your sources carefully. It's not enough to take someone else's word for it. Instead, you need to know where the information comes from and what evidence supports it. If a fact is new or surprising to your audience, it may be worth citing the source to help them to understand why it matters.

Another thing to keep in mind is that not all facts are created equal. Some may be more important or relevant than others, depending on the context of your speech. For example, if you're discussing a current event, you might want to focus on recent developments or breakthroughs rather than long-ago historical events. Similarly, if you're making a persuasive argument, you might choose facts that support your position more strongly than those that don't.

When using historical narratives, it's also important to remember that they are different from historical facts. Historical narratives are stories that recount specific events or experiences, often with an emphasis on drama or emotion. They can be very effective tools for engaging your audience and helping them to understand complex topics, but they should be used sparingly and only when they are relevant to your message.

In terms of length, historical narratives tend to be longer than many other types of supporting materials, such as facts or statistics, as they often involve more detail and require more explanation to fully convey the meaning. However, this doesn't mean that you should avoid using shorter forms of supporting materials altogether—in fact, shorter quotes or anecdotes can be just as effective in capturing your audience's attention and helping them to remember your message.

6. Statistics

Statistic is often misunderstood due to its complexity and the difficulty in understanding the terminology. The very definition of statistic involves collecting, analyzing, comparing, and interpreting numerical data to gain insights and make informed decisions. It is not merely about presenting numerical figures, but about comprehending the patterns, trends, and comparisons that these numbers reveal.

One reason why statistic is often misunderstood is the complexity of the scientific method involved in their application. Terms such as mean, median, and mode can be confusing even for many individuals who are well-versed in mathematics and science. To add to this confusion, concepts like regression analysis, two-tailed T-test, and margin of error can further complicate matters. It is essential to have a solid foundation in these areas before attempting to use statistics in any context, in a speech or in other forms of communication.

Another common misconception about statistics is that they only apply to mathematical models and formulas. While it is true that statistics heavily rely on mathematical principles, it also encompasses real-world scenarios where numerical data is collected and analyzed to make sense of complex phenomena. This includes everything from business and economics to social science and healthcare.

Moreover, people often assume that statistics is all about prediction and forecasting the future based on past trends. While it is true that statistical models can help in forecasting future events, they are not always accurate. The accuracy of predictions depends on various factors such as the quality and quantity of data available, the appropriateness of the model used, and external factors that may influence the outcome. It is crucial to understand that no matter how sophisticated the model is or how much data is available, there will always be a degree of uncertainty associated with statistical predictions.

Statistic is a powerful tool that helps us to make sense of the world by providing valuable insights through numerical data. However, it is essential to understand its true essence and not just focus on its mathematical underpinnings. A basic understanding of statistical terms and concepts is necessary before attempting to use them in any communication setting.

7. Testimonies

Testimony is an essential aspect of many forms of communication, including legal proceedings, academic discussions, and even casual conversations. It refers to other people's words, either quoted or paraphrased, that are used to support a particular point of view or to provide evidence in a case. The use of testimony can greatly enhance the credibility and persuasiveness of a statement, as it often comes from individuals.

When it comes to testimony, it's important to distinguish between two main categories: expert and peer. Expert testimony involves the opinions and interpretations of individuals who possess specialized knowledge or skills related to a particular subject. This could include doctors, lawyers, scientists, engineers, or any other professional with a deep understanding of the topic at hand. Expert testimony is typically considered more reliable than peer testimony.

Peer testimony involves the opinions and experiences of individuals who share similar backgrounds or circumstances as the topic being discussed. This could include family members, friends, or colleagues who can provide valuable insights based on their own experiences. Peer testimony can be just as compelling as expert testimony, especially when it comes to personal stories or anecdotes that help to illustrate a point.

It's important to keep in mind that not all testimonies are created equal. Merely having given testimony in the past does not automatically render your statements trustworthy or credible. The value of a testimony is determined by a range of factors, including the expertise and qualifications of the witness, the credibility of the sources cited, and the relevance and reliability of the information presented.

In addition to providing evidence and supporting arguments, testimony can also serve another important purpose: It can give the audience insight into the feelings and perceptions of others. By sharing their experiences and perspectives, witnesses can help to humanize complex issues and make them more accessible to a wider range of people. This can be particularly useful in cases where there are strong emotions involved or where people may have different cultural or societal beliefs.

8. Quotations

Quotation is a type of supporting materials that are often used to provide evidence or explanation. It belongs to the category of testimony, which is used to support a particular point of view or argument. Quotation is typically used for proof or explanation, as it offers the potential to sway the audience by presenting well-known and respected individuals who express their thoughts and opinions on a given topic.

Quotation can be useful in many different situations, such as in speeches, presentations, or articles. It can help to add credibility and authority to a message by providing the words of respected experts or influential figures. In addition, quotation can also be used to illustrate a point or to make a comparison between two ideas or concepts.

However, there are also some downsides to using quotations in communication. One potential issue is that not all quotations are created equal. That a quote is well-known does not necessarily mean that it is relevant or accurate to the topic being discussed. It's important to carefully consider which quotations to use and ensure that they are appropriate and relevant to the message being conveyed.

Another potential drawback of relying too heavily on quotations is that it can make communication seem dispassionate or impersonal. People are often more likely to be influenced by messages that come from personal experiences or firsthand knowledge rather than generic quotes. While quotes can be useful in providing evidence or explanation, they should be used in conjunction with other forms of supporting materials, such as narratives or examples, to give a more well-rounded and engaging message.

In conclusion, supporting material is an essential part of the successful delivery of speech. It helps to reinforce the main points, provide context and background information, and offer variety and interest to keep the audience engaged throughout the speech. By being selective about the types of supporting materials you use and delivering them effectively, you can ensure that supporting materials can enhance the impact of your presentation.

Exercises

Complete the table according to the Skill Focus in this unit.

Supporting Material Type	Definition	Purpose	Strengths	Weaknesses
Example	_____	To illustrate concepts	Engage audience, clarify ideas	May oversimplify complex topics
Narrative	_____	To convey experiences	Captivate emotions, create empathy	Can be lengthy, lose focus
Definition	Explanation	To clarify terminology	_____	May be dry or too academic
Description	Detailed portrayal	To create mental images	_____	May lack concrete evidence or context
Historical and Scientific Fact	Verifiable data	To provide evidence	_____	May not resonate emotionally with audience

(To be continued)

(Continued)

Supporting Material Type	Definition	Purpose	Strengths	Weaknesses
Statistic	Numerical data	To quantify information	Provide precision, strengthen arguments	_____
Testimony	Personal accounts	To share firsthand information	Add authenticity, humanize content	_____
Quotation	_____	To reinforce statements	Leverage authority, support arguments	May lack originality, context matters

9.3 Speaking Task: Introducing Chinese Architecture

Task Imagine you are tasked with presenting an introduction to Chinese architectural construction to people who are unfamiliar with its unique features. Prepare a speech that emphasizes the distinctive characteristics and aesthetic principles of Chinese architecture and deliver it in the class.

9.4 Self-Reflection: Evaluating the Supporting Materials of Your Speech

Evaluate the supporting materials of your speech based on the information in the following table. Adjust the ratings based on how well you meet each specific criterion, and use it as a tool for providing detailed feedback. Rate your speech on each point: E–excellent, G–good, A–average, F–fair, P–poor.

Checklist: Supporting Materials of Your Speech

Supporting Materials	Scores					Comments
	E	G	A	F	P	
Example						
Narrative						
Definition						
Description						
Historical and scientific fact						
Statistics						
Testimony						
Quotation						

Unit 10

Using Visual Aids Effectively

In this unit you will learn to:

- know different types of visual aids: objects or models, people as visual aids, photographs and drawings, video and audio recordings, charts, graphs, maps, and presentation slides;
- differentiate graphs and charts and understand how to use them effectively in your speech;
- employ the skills of preparing and presenting the visual aids.

 ## 10.1 Speech Reading: Transcending Boundaries

Activity 1 Lead-in Listening

Listen to the speech and complete the blanks with the words in the box.

> test   experimental   taking   absorb   essentially   caffeine

Let me start with the brain and the functions of learning and memory, because what we've discovered over the past 10 or so years is that you need sleep after learning to 1. _____ hit the save button on those new memories so that you don't forget. But recently, we discovered that you also need sleep before learning to actually prepare your brain, almost like a dry sponge ready to initially soak up new information. And without sleep, the memory circuits of the brain essentially become waterlogged, as it were, and you can't 2. _____ new memories. So let me show you the data. Here in this study, we decided to 3. _____ the hypothesis that pulling the all-nighter was a good idea. So we took a group of individuals and we assigned them to one of two 4. _____ groups: a sleep group and a sleep deprivation group. Now the sleep group, they're going to get a full eight hours of slumber, but the deprivation group, we're going to keep them awake in the laboratory under full supervision. There's no nap or 5. _____ by the way, so it's miserable for everyone involved. And then the next day, we're going to place those participants inside an MRI scanner and we're going to have them try and learn a whole list of new facts as we're 6. _____ snapshots of brain activity. And then we're going to test them to see how effective that learning has been. And that's what you're looking at here on the vertical axis. And when you put those two groups head to head, what you find is a quite significant, 40 percent deficit in the ability of the brain to make new memories without sleep.

Activity 2   Pre-reading Questions

1. What do you know about Seamus Heaney?
2. How do you understand the title "Transcending Boundaries"?
3. What do you expect to hear in a commencement address?

Transcending Boundaries[1]

1   The invitation to be your commencement speaker was a great honor but it made me anxious as well. How, I asked myself, can one person address a crowd of 25,000 and hope to establish any kind of worthwhile contact? The odds against it would seem to be high. As a poet, as a member of a large family, as the native of a small country, I know that shared historical experience and shared personal memories and even indeed a shared accent may be necessary before any really credible exchange can take place. I have always loved, for example, the story of the **anthropologist** who was doing field work in a community of the Inuit people living up close to the Arctic circle. Why, the anthropologist asked a wise woman of the tribe: "Why are all your songs so short?" And the wise woman replied, "Our songs are all so short because we know so much." In other words, the experience of living as a single people in a single place, where each new generation follows the same old paths—such an experience produced a wonderful, enviable confidence about the reliability and the knowability of the world.

2   But that experience of living in a closely knit, ethnically **homogeneous**, **hermetically** sealed culture is everywhere a thing of the past. The Amish carriage now shares the highway with the Mercedes car; the Australian bushman may still go walkabout, but he goes connected up to his Walkman; the **recluse** in the beach-hut north of Sausalito may look like a beach-comber, but he is probably an Internet millionaire, scouting his next coup, on his way home to cross the Silicon. Living in the world of the year two thousand means that you inhabit several different **psychic** and cultural levels at the same time. And the marvelous thing about us as

---

[1] This text is adapted from Seamus Heaney's commencement address from the Lanre Dahunsi website.

human beings is that we have been provided with a whole system of intellectual and imaginative elevators that **whisk** us from floor to floor, at will and on **whim**.

3   In the nineteenth century, it was still possible for poets and visionaries to dream that the complications and distractions of modernity could be avoided. Matthew Arnold deplored what he called "the strange disease of modern life / with its sick hurry, its divided aims" and wanted to retreat into the rural beauty of the English countryside. In a similar mood, Henry David Thoreau was drawn to Walden Pond and William Butler Yeats to the Lake Isle of Inn is free. But nowadays, such retreat is hardly possible.

4   You can think about the change positively, of course. If retreat is no longer possible, its loss has been compensated for by boundless opportunities for access. Dreams of unlocking the sites of knowledge and power—dreams that used to be **enshrined** in the words "Open Sesame"①—these have to a large extent been realized in the magic formula. This is the world of globalization where one thing can **impinge** unexpectedly and often drastically upon another; so much so that we no longer have any difficulty in entertaining the theory that the shake of a butterfly's wing in one part of the world is going to produce a tornado in another. And this is the world that commences for you in earnest after this commencement. Today is the moment of ritual separation from what was for a while a reliable and relatively knowable world. We can think of it as a rite of passage from the nest to the sky, from the dens where you were fended for into the fields where you will have to fend for yourself. No wonder there is an out of the ordinariness about this morning's ceremonies.

5   There is a dream-like quality to every commencement day. But the veil trembles more mysteriously if you are graduating in the year 2000. It makes you wonder if the date is a destiny or an accident. A turning point in your life has coincided with a turning point in our era. It is like the moment when a tide has risen to its highest and then rests: everything is at the full and yet everything is **volatile**. And for the duration of this moment, you are held between two worlds. It's like those few seconds when you pause and hold the pose, and are photographed standing between your parents and your professors.

6   Today, inevitably, many of you will experience this in-between condition. You stand at a boundary. Behind you is your natural habitat, as it were, the grounds of your creaturely being, the old haunts where you were nurtured; in front of you is a less knowable prospect of invitation and challenge, the testing ground of your possibilities. You stand between whatever binds you to your past and whatever might be unbounded in your future.

7   One kind of wisdom says, keep your feet on the ground. Be faithful to the ancestors. Remember the short songs of the wise woman. Another says, lift up your

eyes. Spread your wings. Don't **renege** on the other world you have been shown. One kind of wisdom says if you change your language, you betray your origins. Another kind says all language is preparation for further language. All of you are likely to be caught between these conflicting wisdoms and indeed you are unlikely ever to be able to choose confidently between them, now or in the future. And so my advice to you is to understand that this in-between condition is not to be regarded as a disabling confusion but that it is rather a necessary state, a consequence of our situation between earthy origin and angelic potential.

...

> **Analysis**
>
> The speech is a commencement address delivered by Seamus Heaney, who is recognized as one of the most important poets of the 20th century, in 2000 to the graduates of the University of Pennsylvania. It presents a thoughtful reflection on the challenges and opportunities faced by graduates in a rapidly changing and interconnected world.
>
> The presenter, presumed to be a commencement speaker, establishes his credibility by referring to the honor of being invited to address the graduates. The presenter's experience as a poet and his understanding of shared experiences and cultural diversity lend authority to his words.
>
> The speech evokes a sense of nostalgia and uncertainty as it describes the transition from the "reliable and relatively knowable world", to a more unpredictable and dynamic future. The presenter captures the emotions graduates might feel as they stand on the threshold of a new phase in their lives. The comparison to standing between parents and professors in a photograph highlights the sense of being caught between two worlds and the bittersweet nature of this moment.
>
> The speech employs logical appeals by addressing the realities of the modern world, where cultural and technological boundaries have blurred. It acknowledges the loss of the possibility of retreat to a simpler and more rural life, highlighting the need to adapt to the complexities of the contemporary globalized world. That the world has become interconnected and that even small actions can have far-reaching consequences are logical arguments for the challenges and opportunities faced by the graduates.
>
> Overall, the speech conveys a message of embracing the in-between condition that graduates find themselves in. It encourages them to navigate the balance between preserving their cultural heritage and embracing new experiences, languages, and opportunities. The presenter suggests that this in-between state is not a source of confusion but a necessary aspect of personal growth and adaptation to the changing world.

Useful Words & Expressions

anthropologist	n.	人类学家
enshrine	v.	视……为神圣；珍藏
hermetically	adv.	与外界隔绝地，不受外界干扰地
homogeneous	adj.	同种类的，同性质的
impinge	v.	影响，冲击
psychic	adj.	超自然的，通灵的
recluse	n.	隐居者
renege	v.	食言，反悔
volatile	adj.	易变的，动荡不定的
whim	n.	心血来潮，突发奇想
whisk	v.	搅动

Note

Open Sesame: It is from the Arabian folk tale collection "One Thousand and One Nights", specifically in the story of "Ali Baba and the Forty Thieves". It is the magic phrase the thieves use to open the door to their treasure-filled cave.

Critical Thinking

1. How should a speaker adapt his or her use of visual aids based on the audience's characteristics, such as age, cultural background, or prior knowledge? What considerations should be taken into account when tailoring aids to the audience?

2. How do visual aids give a speaker more confidence in his or her presentation? What is the relationship between a speaker's confidence and the effectiveness of his or her message?

3. When using visual aids, what ethical considerations should a speaker keep in mind? How can a speaker ensure his or her using these aids responsibly and not misleading the audience?

4. How should a speaker select the most appropriate visual aids for his or her message? What criteria should he or she consider to ensure the aids are effective and enhance the speech?

5. If a speaker is set to present on the topic of "Transcending Boundaries", what visual aids can he or she employ to enhance the presentation's impact?

10.2 Skill Focus: Using Visual Aids Effectively

Visual aids are the resources beyond the words that you can use to enhance the message conveyed to the audience, which include pictures, diagrams, charts, graphs, maps, presentation slides, and the like. When used properly, visual aids can enhance the impact of a speech, increase the persuasiveness of a speech, heighten audience interest, and give the speaker more confidence in the presentation.

10.2.1 Kinds of Visual Aids

1. Objects or Models

Objects and models are forms of the visual aids that can be very helpful in conveying the message to the audience. Objects refer to something you can hold up and talk about during the speech, which are more direct and vivid.

If the object is too big or too small, or sometimes unavailable, you can prepare a model, usually built to scale to represent the object in detail. When presenting an object or a model, you should not pass it around during the speech because it is highly distracting.

2. People as Visual Aids

A speaker can often use his or her own body to demonstrate facets of a speech. Doing some kinds of demonstration can help the speaker to clarify the points, and at the same time, it can arouse the audience's interest and keep them involved. If the speaker wants to demonstrate perfectly during the speech, he or she need to practice in advance to coordinate his or her actions with his or her words, and meanwhile to maintain eye contact with the audience.

In some cases, it is necessary to ask someone else to serve as the visual aid. If you are the speaker, you should arrange ahead of time for a person (or persons) to act as the effective aid. You cannot assume that an audience member will volunteer on the spot. If you plan to demonstrate how to perform an acupuncture therapy, your volunteer must know in advance what you will do on him and consent to do so.

3. Photographs and Drawings

Sometimes photographs or drawings are the best ways to show an unfamiliar but important detail. You had better choose large-size photographs or drawings which can be easily and clearly seen by the audience. Normal-size photographs are too small to be seen without passing around, which will distract the audience's attention from what you are saying. Another effective way is to put photographs or drawings on presentation slides, and they should be relevant and not detract from the message of the slide.

4. Video or Audio Recordings

Video or audio recordings are another useful types of visual aids. When used properly, they can enhance your speech.

There is one major warning to using audio or video recordings during a speech: Do not forget that they are supposed to be aids to the speech, not the speech itself. The video can never overshadow the speech. In addition, be sure to avoid the mistakes that speakers often make.

First, avoid choosing clips that are too long for the overall length of the speech. It's apparently inappropriate that you insert a one-minute video clip in a five-minute speech. Usually, a 30-second video can help to illustrate your point in an impressive way. Something much longer may cause more harm than good.

Second, practice with the audio or video equipment before the speech. If you are unfamiliar with the equipment, you'll look inexperienced trying to figure out how it works, and it also wastes valuable time of the audience. Therefore, it is necessary to check the equipment and be sure it works properly and the video looks fine when projected on a large screen.

Finally, cue the clip to the appropriate place before beginning your speech. Don't search in panic for the part you need to play during the speech. You need to make sure your video is ready to start exactly when you want it. If necessary, edit the video to the precise length you need so it will blend smoothly into your speech. Moreover, you should give the audience the context before a video or audio clip is played, specifically what the clip is and why it relates to the speech. At the same time, the video should not repeat what you have already said, but instead add new information to it.

5. Charts

A chart is commonly defined as a graphical representation of data (often numerical) or a sketch representing an ordered process. Chart is especially useful for summarizing large blocks of information. It is important to use charts which exactly match the specific purpose in your speech.

Charts usually fall into three types: statistical charts, sequence-of-steps charts, and decision trees.

1) Statistical Charts

Statistical charts must be kept as simple as possible, and the data should be explained. When you visually display information from a quantitative study, you should make sure that you understand the material and you can successfully explain the data. Another factor to consider is the educational background of the audience, that is, how well the data can be accessible to the audience. If you deliver a speech to an upper-level graduates or professionals who understand statistical analysis, then the chart is appropriate. Otherwise, avoid being too technical and try to explain the data in a simpler and more familiar way.

2) Sequence-of-Steps Charts

Sequence-of-steps charts are useful when you are trying to explain a process that involves several steps. They show the specific steps vividly and directly, which are powerful visual aids when delivering a speech.

3) Decision Trees

Decision trees are useful to show the relationships among ideas. They are utilized for both classification and regression tasks. For example, a sequence-of-step chart has a hierarchical, tree structure, which consists of a root node, branches, internal nodes, and leaf nodes. Like other types of charts, you should make sure that the information in the decision tree is relevant to the purpose of your speech and that each question is clearly labeled.

6. Graphs

Graphs are used to show statistical trends and patterns, which focus more on how one factor (such as size, weight, and the number of items) varies in comparison to other items. A graph is a pictorial representation of the relationships of quantitative data using dots, lines, bars, pie slices, and the like. You can show graphs using a range of different formats. Some of these formats are specialized for various professional fields. Graphs commonly used in the speech are line graphs, bar graphs, pie graphs, and pictographs.

1) Line Graphs

A line graph is one that uses one or more lines to show changes of data over time or space. It is informative in allowing people to visualize trends. Line graphs can be classified into two types. The first one is a single line graph in which only one dependent variable is tracked, so there is only a single line connecting all data points on the graph, which relate to the same item, and the only purpose of the graph is to track the changes of that variable over time.

The other one is a multiple graph. More than one dependent variable is tracked on the graph and compared over a single independent variable (often time). Different dependent variables are often given different colored lines to distinguish data sets.

2) Bar Graphs

A bar graph uses vertical or horizontal bars to show comparisons among two or more items. Bar graphs are useful for showing the differences between quantities, which can facilitate the comparisons among different items and make the differences strikingly noticeable to the audience.

3) Pie Graphs

A pie graph is usually depicted as a circle and is designed to show proportional relationships within the sets of data. In other words, it shows the parts or percentages of a whole. A pie graph should be simplified as much as possible without eliminating important information. Compared with other graphs, the sections of the pie need to be plotted proportionally.

When you use pie graphs to dramatize relationships among the parts of a whole, you should keep the number of segments in the graph as small as possible. In most cases, it ranges from two to five. Rarely does a pie graph have more than eight segments. The graph with many segments is illegible, confusing, and overwhelming in every way because it contains too much information and is more likely to confuse the audience than to help them to understand the information of your speech.

4) Pictograph

Similar to a bar graph, a pictograph uses numbers and/or sizes of iconic symbols to dramatize differences in amounts. Pictograph does not allow for the depiction of specific statistical data.

7. Maps

A map is extremely useful if the information is clear and limited. There are different kinds of maps, including population, weather, ocean current, political, and economic maps, so you should choose the right kind of map that emphasizes the information you need to deliver, for the purpose of your speech.

8. Presentation Slides

As for presentation slides, the most commonly known one is PowerPoint. Presentation slides allow the visualization of concepts, and can be embedded with videos and audio, and words can be input on the screen. Here are some tips for you to prepare the presentation slides.

(1) Consistency is the first rule you need to remember. It is best to use a single

font for the text on your visuals so that it looks like a unified set. Or you can use two different fonts in consistent ways, such as having all headings and titles in the same font and all bullet points in the same font. Additionally, you'd better keep the background consistent, whether it is the design template or background color you choose.

(2) Remember to keep your presentation slides simple and clear. Each slide should have one message, one photo, and one graphic. The audience should know what they are supposed to see on the slide. Avoid putting too much information on a slide. The standard rule is for text 7×7, or sometimes (if the screen is smaller) 6×6. It means, in the case of 7×7, you should have no more than seven horizontal lines of text (including the heading) and the longest line should not exceed seven words. Nor should you prepare too many slides. Usually a ten-minute speech probably needs fewer than ten slides.

(3) Visibility is another factor you need to consider. Text should not be smaller than 22 point font for best visibility. Experts recommend using at least 44-point type for titles, 36-point type for subtitles, and 28-point type for other texts. High contrast between the text and background is extremely important. White fonts against dark backgrounds and black fonts against light backgrounds are probably the best choice. Avoid putting words on photos, which make the words difficult to read. A more effective method is to place the text beneath the image to enhance clarity and ensure the text is easily readable.

10.2.2 Preparing Presentation Aids

Here are some tips to prepare presentation aids, which can help you to design presentation aids more effectively and more visually appealing.

On one hand, keep the presentation aids simple, clear and to the point, which contain enough information to communicate your point, but not so many to confuse or distract the audience. Avoid elaborate presentation aids overly. Instead, simplify them as much as possible, emphasizing the information you want the audience to understand. Misspellings, mistakes and poorly designed presentation aids should be avoided because they can damage your credibility.

On the other hand, make sure presentation aids are large enough to be seen by the audience in the room. You can check its visibility in advance by walking around the room. If people sitting in the most distant place can see it, the size of the presentation aids is acceptable. And use the fonts that are easy to read. Avoid decorative fonts (a font with exaggerated features like exaggerated serifs, swishes, curls, or calligraphic lines) because they are hard to read and are distracting. In addition, presentation aids should be aesthetically pleasing. The presentation aids should be unified and consistent in tone and style, and they should have a focal point and use garish colors, helping to deliver important message in a pleasing way.

In one word, whatever the presentation aid is, it should support your speech and have high relevance to your speech content. It works as an aid, helping to clarify the message, emphasize the importance of an idea, and improve the audience's understanding.

10.2.3 Presenting Visual Aids

When presenting visual aids, you should take the following tips into consideration.

(1) Displaying visual aids where the audience can see them without straining. Be sure to place the visual aid where it can be easily seen by everyone in the room. When you are discussing the visual aid, stand to one side and point to it. Wherever you put the visual aid, remember not to obstruct the audience's view.

(2) Explaining visual aids. When you present a visual aid in your speech, you need to explain what it shows, point out, and name the most important features. You need to let the audience know what to look for, rather than rushing over visual aids without any explanation.

(3) Avoiding passing visual aids among the audience. If you pass visual aids among the audience, their attention will be quickly distracted from your speech to the visual aids. The same is true of handouts. Sometimes, you prepare a handout for the audience, and then you may notice they spend a good deal of time looking over the handout, rather than listening to the speech, so the best time to distribute the handout is at the end of your speech when you have finished talking.

(4) Displaying visual aids only when discussing them. You cannot display the visual aids throughout your speech because they are distracting. Display the visual aid when you are ready to discuss it. Keep it out of sight when you finish your discussion.

(5) Talking to your audience, not to the visual aid. When explaining a visual aid, you still need to keep eye contact with the audience. You can glance at the visual aid periodically, but your eyes still fix upon the audience. Therefore, you can notice the feedback about how the visual aid and your explanation are coming across, and then make timely adjustment.

Unit 10 Using Visual Aids Effectively

Exercises

I. Decide whether the following statements are TRUE (T), FALSE (F) or NOT GIVEN (NG) according to the Skill Focus in this unit.

1. People find a speaker's message more interesting, grasp it more easily, and retain it longer when it is presented visually as well as verbally. (   )
2. A speaker uses graphs to show statistical trends and patterns, which can help the audience to catch on to a complex series of numbers. (   )
3. A line graph is better than a pie graph in dramatizing relationships among the parts of a whole. (   )
4. A bar graph highlights the segments of a circle to show simple distribution patterns. (   )
5. Charts are especially useful for summarizing large blocks of information, and you should list more than ten items in a single chart. (   )
6. Speakers can use their body as a visual aid by performing actions. When doing a demonstration, speakers need to coordinate their actions with their words and to maintain eye contact with the audience. (   )
7. When you use the presentation slides in your speech, you can put everything you say on the screen for the audience to read. (   )
8. Using all capital letters on a visual aid can highlight the message and make it easier to read. (   )
9. A video can work well if it is limited in length, carefully edited, and skillfully worked into the speech. (   )
10. Visual aids should be displayed before you begin your speech. (   )

II. Choose the best options to answer the following questions or fill in the blanks according to the information given in this unit.

1. _____ is a particularly good way to show comparisons between two or among more items.
   A. A bar graph
   B. A line graph
   C. A pie graph
   D. A chart

2. Which of the following statements about the chart is TRUE?
   A. Chart is especially useful for summarizing large blocks of information.

B. When using a chart, you can include as much information as possible.

C. To include more information, lists on a chart should exceed ten items.

D. Chart is more direct and clearer in presenting information than graph.

3. The following are the principles for using videos as a visual aid EXCEPT that _____.

   A. the video must be limited in length and cannot be too long

   B. the speaker makes sure the video is cued to start exactly where you want it

   C. the video is edited to the precise length you need so it will blend smoothly into your speech

   D. a 10-minute high-resolution video is a good fit for any speech

4. Which of the following statements about the use of presentation slides is TRUE?

   A. Speakers can use presentation slides to illustrate every point of their talk.

   B. Speakers need a clear idea of exactly why, how and when to use presentation slides in the speech.

   C. Using presentation slides can save much preparation time for speech making.

   D. Speakers should limit their slides to no more than a dozen lines of type.

5. When you prepare the visual aids, you should _____.

   A. use decorative fonts to make them visually appealing

   B. use all capital letters to make them more noticeable

   C. use colors thoughtfully and strategically

   D. use multiple aids such as combining presentation slides with objects and models

6. When you design visual aids, we should make them _____.

   A. simple

   B. clear to the point

   C. visually appealing

   D. all of the above

7. Which of the following behaviors should be avoided?

   A. Check the speech room in advance to decide where you display your visual aids more effectively.

   B. Explain your visual aids when presenting them in your speech.

   C. Pass visual aids among the audience in the speech.

   D. Develop a backup plan in case there are problems with your visual aids on the day of the speech.

8. When can you display your visual aids?

   A. Display them while you are discussing them.

B. Display them throughout the whole speech.
C. Display them when you finish discussing.
D. Display them before you are ready to discuss them.

9. When explaining a visual aid, you should _____.
   A. keep your eyes fixed on the visual aid
   B. look primarily at the aid, and glance at your audience occasionally
   C. keep eye contact with the audience
   D. glance at the aid periodically or look elsewhere

10. What can you do to practice with your visual aids?
    A. Rehearse when or how you will show your aids.
    B. Control the timing of each move.
    C. Integrate your visual aids perfectly with your words.
    D. All of the above.

10.3 Speaking Task: Making a Speech with Visual Aids

Task Deliver a persuasive speech organized in problem-solution order or problem-cause-solution order. Pay attention to the visual aids you use in your speech. The following outline is for your reference.

Central idea: The lack of regular physical activity is a significant health issue affecting productivity and well-being in the workplace. Companies should implement programs that encourage healthy exercise habits among the employees.

Main Points:
1. The impact of the sedentary lifestyle on employee health.
2. Benefits of the workplace exercise programs

10.4 Self-Reflection: Evaluating Your Speech in Using Visual Aids

Evaluate your speech based on the rubrics for assessing your speech in using visual aids. Rate your speech on each point: E—excellent, G—good, A—average, F—fair, P—poor.

Checklist: Using Visual Aids

Items	Scores					Comments
	E	G	A	F	P	
Did you introduce the topic clearly?						
Did you establish credibility?						
Visual aids used						
Visual aids organization (1) the placement (2) the use of color						
Visual aids effectiveness (1) conveying the message (2) engaging the audience						
Visual aids integration (1) their relevance to the topic (2) their ability to support the main points						
Visual aids creativity (1) their originality (2) their ability to capture the audience's attention						
Are the visual aids clear, simple and easily readable?						
Did you present the visual aids effectively?						
Did you reinforce the central idea in the conclusion?						

Unit 11

Talking to Your Audience

In this unit you will learn to:

- get to know the different kinds of speech delivery;
- learn to use non-verbal strategies when delivering a speech;
- make successful online speech deliveries;
- respond to messages emotionally, cognitively, and behaviorally and "co-create" them;
- deliver speeches with dignity and grace.

11.1 Speech Reading: Education for Sustainable Development

Activity 1 Lead-in Listening

Listen to the speech and answer the following questions.

What are the implications (both positive and negative) of Boeing's moving up the engine on the wing of 737, as seen in the redesign for the 737 Max series?

Activity 2 Pre-reading Questions

1. What is the role of education in society? In your opinion, what are the core purposes of education?

2. Horace Mann, a well-known American educator, stated that education is "a great equalizer of conditions of men". In your opinion, what possible biases could education help to equalize?

Education for Sustainable Development[1]

1   It gives me a great pleasure to join you for this important **initiative** as the UN

---

1 This text is adapted from the speech of Madame Peng Liyuan, wife of Chinese President Xi Jinping, at the UNESCO World Conference on Education for Sustainable Development.

marks its 70th anniversary.

2   Education is very close in my heart. My father grew up in a very small village in China. In those days, not many villagers could read. So my father opened a night school to teach them how to read. With his help, many people learned to write their own names; with his help, many people learned to read newspapers for the first time; with his help, many women were able to teach their children how to read. As his daughter, I know what education means to the people, especially those without it.

3   After generations of hard work, China has come a long way in education. I, myself, am a **beneficiary** of that progress. Otherwise, I would never have become a **soprano** and a professor of music. I am following my father's footsteps by teaching at China's Conservatory of Music to help continue China's success story.

4   I want to thank Director-general Bokova and UNESCO for naming me the Special Envoy for the Advancement of Girls' and Women's Education. I am truly honored to work with the UN and do something about Global Education. I have visited many schools around the world. I've seen first-hand on how much we can do for education.

5   Education is about women and girls. It is important for girls to go to school because they will become their children's first teacher someday. But women still account for over half of the world's poor in population and 60% of adults who can't read. Education is crucial in the addressing such inequalities. In China, the Spring Bud Education Program[①] has helped over 3 million girls go back to school. Many of them have finished university education and they are doing well at work.

6   Education is about equality. In poor countries and regions, the number of school **drop-outs** is astonishing. We call for more educational resources to these places.

7   Education is about the young people. Young people are the future. Education is important because it not only gives young people knowledge and skills but also helps them become responsible citizens.

8   As the UNESCO special envoy and the mother myself, my commitment to education for all will never change. Many years ago, my father made a small difference in his village. Together, we can make a big difference in the world.

9   I was once asked about my Chinese dream. I said I hope all children, especially girls, can have access to good education. This is my Chinese dream. I believe one day education first will no longer be a dream but a reality enjoyed by every young woman on this planet.

> **Analysis**
>
> The speech discusses the importance of education, particularly for women and girls.

The presenter shares a personal story about her father's efforts to teach literacy in a small village in China and highlights the impact education had on the villagers. The presenter, as a beneficiary of education, explains her role as a soprano and a professor of music and expresses gratitude for being named the Special Envoy for the Advancement of Girls' and Women's Education by UNESCO. The presenter emphasizes the significance of education for women, addressing inequalities, promoting equality, and empowering young people. She shares examples of successful education initiatives in China and advocates for more resources to be allocated to education in underserved regions. The presenter concludes by stating the commitment to promoting education for all and expressing their dream that every young woman worldwide will have access to quality education.

The argument in the speech is effectively presented through the use of supporting evidence, personal anecdotes, and a clear call to action. The presenter begins with a personal story about her father's efforts to illustrate the transformative power of education and set the context for the importance of the topic. This anecdote serves as the compelling evidence of the positive impact that education can have on individuals and communities.

Throughout the speech, the presenter uses statistics and real-world examples to support her claims. For instance, she mentions the Spring Bud Education Program in China that has helped millions of girls to return to school and has achieved success. By referencing specific initiatives and outcomes, the presenter adds credibility to her argument and demonstrates that progress is possible.

The presenter's role as a UNESCO Special Envoy lends further credibility to her message, as China have been tasked with a significant responsibility related to education. By sharing the personal commitment and dreams for universal education, the presenter creates an emotional connection with the audience. Her statement that education "is not only a dream, it will be a reality enjoyed by every young woman on this planet" resonates as a strong and aspirational call to action.

Overall, the speech effectively combines personal stories, evidence, and a passionate call for action to advocate for education, particularly for women and girls. The presenter's credibility, emotional appeal, and well-supported points make the argument persuasive and compelling.

Useful Words

beneficiary	n.	受益者
drop-out	n.	退学

initiative	n.	措施；倡议
soprano	n.	女高音
sustainable	adj.	可持续的

Note

the Spring Bud Education Program: In 1989, under the leadership of the All-China Women's Federation, the China Children and Teenagers' Fund launched the "Spring Bud Education Program", a public welfare initiative dedicated to improving the educational conditions of girls from impoverished families. For a long time, with the attention and care of the Party and the government, and the active participation and generous donations from all sectors of society, the "Spring Bud Education Program" has carried out various forms of care and assistance around girls' education, safety, and health, helping a large number of Spring Bud girls to pursue their dreams of learning and to grow and succeed.

Critical Thinking

1. How do nonverbal strategies enhance the engagement and clarity of a speech? What specific nonverbal cues can the speaker use to make his or her presentation more compelling?

2. What are the specific considerations for delivering a speech online? How do these considerations differ from those of in-person presentations? How can the speaker adapt his or her skills accordingly?

3. What new opportunities and challenges does technology present for speakers?

4. What are the common strengths and weaknesses of different speaking styles?

5. How do personal speaking styles influence the impact of a speech within "Education First for Sustainable Development"?

11.2 Skill Focus: Talking to Your Audience

There's no perfect way to give a speech. You all have your own unique speaking styles with different strengths, but there are strategies you can employ to engage your audience, keep them interested, and get your message across more clearly.

In this unit, four basic styles of speech presentation will be introduced. Next, non-verbal strategies to make speech more engaging will be listed. Finally, specific considerations for online delivery will be discussed.

11.2.1 Delivery Style

There are four basic ways or styles of speech delivery: manuscript, memorized, impromptu, and extemporaneous. Each style will work well in different conversational contexts.

1. Manuscript

As for manuscript, a speech is written and the presenter reads it word for word to the audience. This style is common among news anchors and television personalities. To those unfamiliar with teleprompters and manuscripts, it sounds lofty and boring. Public speaking is not reading aloud but presenting in front of an audience. For this reason, manuscript styles are always used in specific situations and not in instructional speeches. Manuscript is used mainly for accuracy. Also, facts and names in a manuscript must be accurate and precise so that there is no room for error.

2. Memorized

This style of speech is used when you memorize your manuscript and present it word by word to your audience. In this kind of speech delivery, you will focus too much on remembering what's next instead of focusing on the audience. Your focus is inward, making this sound robotic and drab. Therefore, you had better memorize the main points rather than every single word of the speech.

3. Impromptu

An impromptu speech is usually a short presentation without prior preparation. An impromptu speech often occurs when someone is asked to "say a few words" or toast to a special occasion. The advantage of this style of speech delivery is that it tends to be spontaneous and conveys the message in a more natural and chatty way. The downside is that the presenter is given little time to think about the central issue or organize the message. As a result, the message may be disjointed and difficult for the audience to understand.

4. Extemporaneous

This style of speech delivery is carefully planned, rehearsed, and delivered in conversation using short notes. Speaking off the cuff has many advantages. This increases your chances of being perceived as competent and trustworthy as a speaker. Additionally, your message has both verbal and non-verbal appeal, so the audience is more likely to pay more attention to your message.

Speaking extemporaneously and spontaneously requires a lot of preparation for both the verbal and non-verbal components of speech. The day before a scheduled lecture is not sufficient for preparation. The key to this style of speech is that it is carefully planned to look natural and conversational.

There are several ways you can choose to give your speech, but the simplest approach isn't always the best. It takes a lot of work to prepare an effective speech. You should learn how to connect with your audience and build confidence in the process. Speaking allows meaningful pauses, eye contact, small changes in word order, and emphasis in the voice. Reading is the more or less exact representation of words on paper without the use of non-verbal interpretation.

11.2.2 Non-verbal Strategies

Your abilities and perceptions help to determine how interactions unfold and whether they actually occur. But non-verbal cues make up a lot of the content from which you get your first impressions, so it's important to understand the fact that people make judgments about your identities and abilities from the very short exposures. Therefore, you should pay attention to non-verbal strategies, which can be used to deliver a speech, such as strategies about appearance and body language.

1. Appearance

Appearance is often the easiest way to build (or destroy) your credibility as a speaker. Your appearance is the first and the most obvious thing your audience will notice while you are giving a speech. Showcasing your positive side through your clothing and grooming can provide much confidence in your abilities. Here are some tips you can follow: (1) Dress for the occasion. Consider dressing appropriately for the speech and the culture of the audience. (2) Keep eye contact with the audience. You have to look a step above your audience. (3) Consider your purpose and what impression you want to make on the audience.

2. Body Language

Your overall movement is an integral part of being a successful speaker. Posture, gesture, and facial expression can be loosely categorized as body language. Body language should be relaxed, natural and purposeful. The following are how to use body language effectively.

Stand up tall! Posture is actually very important. When you stand tall, you are telling your audience, without saying a word, that you are in a position of power and that you take your position seriously. While you often find yourself in a more relaxed position (especially for longer sessions, such as a 90-minute lecture), it's always a good idea to start by standing up straight and putting your best foot forward. Remember, you only have one chance to make the first impression. Your body alignment is one of the first pieces of information your audience uses to make the first impression.

An open posture conveys a friendly and positive attitude. Showing your palms can indicate an open posture, especially when your hands are relaxed. Relaxed yet professional body and head positioning give a confident impression. All you have to do is to practice open posture in front of a mirror so you can see what your audience will see and to practice an open posture with your camera to see what your audience will see.

Unless you're stuck behind a podium because you have to use a static microphone, don't stand in the same spot during your speech. Movement during speech should not resemble tempo.

Movements that support delivery include: turning your torso toward the audience so that you can connect with your audience by leaning slightly towards them; transition steps—every time you transition from one idea to the next, you can go through a few steps; standing still and showing interest when listening to a question; getting closer to the visual which can help to draw the viewer's attention where you need it.

Gestures are forms of non-verbal communication in which visible physical actions convey specific messages. Effective gestures are intentional and natural. The following are gestures to support your message: (1) an emblem is a gesture with a specific meaning. It is often used in place of verbal communication such as waving. It can be used as an aid in telling a story or to emphasize dramatic points during a speech.(2) illustrator helps to emphasize and explain words. Illustrator is the most common type of gesture and is used to illustrate the verbal message that accompanies it. (3) emote displays show emotions and feelings. (4) regulators are gestures that help to regulate the flow of conversation. If you want the audience to answer a question, nod or wave to indicate that you're giving them the "presenter" role.

In order to have the gestures make sense, you can take the following tips into consideration. Make sure the audience can see your hands. You can use targeted gestures while practicing voice memos and keep hands-free. They create more opportunities for spontaneous gestures. Meanwhile, gestures should be natural and not overly flashy or understated. Arm gestures and fists may undermine the message and reduce credibility. And not using gestures may waste the opportunity to suggest emphasis, enthusiasm, or other personal connection to the topic. In addition, emotions should also be taken into consideration. There are seven commonly accepted emotions: fear, anger, surprise, contempt, disgust, happiness and sadness.

When delivering a speech, you should also pay attention to eye contact with the audience. Public speaking is a dialog, not a monologue. Here are the tips for practicing eye contact with the audience: (1) You can use some objects to practice with and get used to looking directly at what's in the audience's path. (2) Take turns talking to spectators to your right, left, and in front of you. (3) Practice with people. Of course, recording yourself, talking to a wall, or talking to a mirror can also help. (4) Do not leave notes on the screen during the presentation.

11.2.3 Online Speech Delivery

Virtual presentation have emerged as a powerful tool that connects individuals with the audience worldwide. Whether you are delivering a webinar, conducting an online workshop, or giving a virtual conference speech, mastering the art of online speech delivery is not just a skill, but also a necessity. While the foundational principles of effective online presentations remain applicable in both in-person and virtual contexts, online speech delivery comes with its own unique challenges and considerations that require special attention. In this part, we will delve into the significance of online speech delivery and offer essential tips for successful online speech delivery.

1. The Significance of Online Speech Delivery

1) Global Reach

Through the online speech delivery, you can share your insights, knowledge, and ideas with the audience from diverse backgrounds and cultures in the world.

2) Convenience

The online speech delivery redefines convenience for both presenters and attendees. As a presenter, you can reach your audience without the need for extensive travel, and attendees can participate by phones or computers.

3) Cost-Efficiency

The cost-efficiency of the online speech delivery is undeniable. Hosting virtual events can eliminate expense related to travel, accommodation, and venue rentals.

4) Accessibility

The online speech delivery fosters inclusivity by making content accessible to individuals with disabilities or mobility challenges. This aligns with the principles of diversity and inclusion, ensuring that your message reaches a broader audience.

5) Time Efficiency

The online speech delivery can save both presenters and attendees valuable time by eliminating the need for travel. This allows participants to focus on engaging with content rather than navigating logistical details.

2. Essential Tips for Successful Online Speech Delivery

While the benefits of the online speech delivery are clear, achieving success in this format requires careful planning, engaging content creation, and impeccable delivery. Here are essential tips to consider when you prepare to captivate the audience.

1) Understand Your Audience

As with any presentation, audience understanding is the key. Tailor your content to address their needs, interests, and expectations. Get to know the audience to prepare the content that resonates deeply with them.

2) Engaging Content Creation

The virtual space demands captivating content that grabs the audience's attention from the start. Utilize storytelling, anecdotes, and relatable examples to illustrate your points and maintain the engagement throughout your online presentation.

3) Effective Use of Visual Aids

Visual aids, such as presentation slides, videos, and graphics, play a vital role in enhancing the impact of your presentation. Keep your visual of your online speech delivery aids clean, visually appealing, and directly aligned with the core messages of your online speech delivery.

4) Foster Audience Interaction

Incorporate interactive elements to sustain the audience engagement. Polls, Q&A sessions, and interactive exercises provide participants with a sense of involvement, making your online speech delivery a dynamic and inclusive experience.

5) Dynamic Delivery

The quality of your online speech delivery significantly influences the effectiveness of your presentation. You can speak clearly, vary your tone of voice, and use gestures to emphasize key points.

6) Virtual Eye Contact

Keep virtual eye contact by looking directly into your camera. This simple act creates a powerful sense of connection, making your audience feel as though you are addressing them personally.

7) Leverage Non-verbal Communication

Non-verbal cues remain impactful in the online speech presentation. You should maintain an open posture and use appropriate gestures to convey enthusiasm and engagement.

8) Thorough Rehearsal

Practicing your presentation many times is crucial. Familiarize yourself with the equipment you will use and rehearse with it to ensure a smooth and confident delivery.

9) Technical Preparedness

Familiarize yourself with the virtual platform, test your microphone, camera, and screen sharing functionalities, and have a backup plan ready.

10) Create an Optimal Environment

Choose a quiet, well-lit space for your presentation. Your background should be free of distractions and contribute to a professional and focused atmosphere.

11) Effective Use of Speech Notes

Prepare concise speech notes that serve as a guiding framework rather than a verbatim script. Tape your notes near your camera or screen to minimize distractions and maintain connection with your audience.

12) Facilitate Audience Engagement

Encourage active participation from the audience. Address questions, acknowledge comments, and make the audience feel valued and heard.

13) Adapt to Audience Feedback

Pay attention to audience reactions and adapt your pacing, content, or delivery based on their engagement level and response.

14) Self-Assessment Through Recording

If possible, record your presentation for self-assessment. Review the recording to identify room for the improvement in the online speech delivery.

15) Dress Professionally

Your appearance remains important in a virtual setting. Dress professionally and align your attire with the tone and nature of your presentation.

16) Maintain Composure

Technical hiccups or unexpected interruptions may occur. Stay composed and have contingency plans in place to handle such situations gracefully.

In conclusion, in the ever-evolving landscape of communication, the online speech delivery has emerged as a potent medium for connecting and inspiring the audience around the world. Mastering the intricacies of the online speech delivery demands a combination of meticulous preparation, engaging content creation, and effective delivery skills.

Exercises

Choose the best options to answer the following questions or fill in the blanks according to the Skill Focus in this unit.

1. Which of the following is NOT one of the four basic styles of speech delivery discussed in the article?
   A. Spontaneous.   B. Manuscript.
   C. Extemporaneous.   D. Memorized.

2. Which delivery style involves reading a speech word for word from a written text, often using a teleprompter?
   A. Impromptu.   B. Extemporaneous.
   C. Manuscript.   D. Memorized.

3. Manuscript speeches are often used by news anchors and television personalities because _____.
   A. they are more engaging and spontaneous.
   B. they allow for improvisation and creativity.
   C. they ensure accuracy and precision of information.
   D. they promote natural and chatty communication.

4. Which style of speech delivery involves memorizing the entire speech and presenting it verbatim?
   A. Impromptu.   B. Extemporaneous.
   C. Manuscript.   D. Memorized.

5. What is one drawback of using memorization to deliver a speech?
   A. It requires extensive use of notes and prompts.
   B. It often results in a lack of audience engagement.
   C. It can lead to the overuse of gestures and body language.
   D. It hinders the speaker's ability to focus on their audience.

6. Which style of speech delivery is characterized by spontaneity and little to no prior preparation?
   A. Manuscript.   B. Extemporaneous.
   C. Impromptu.   D. Memorized.

7. An impromptu speech might be more natural and engaging for an audience because _____.
   A. it relies on pre-written scripts for accurate delivery
   B. it allows the speaker to use memorized gestures
   C. it conveys a message in a spontaneous and conversational manner
   D. it involves meticulous planning and rehearsal

8. What is the key advantage of using extemporaneous speech delivery?
   A. It requires minimal preparation and planning.
   B. It allows the speaker to read from a manuscript.
   C. It ensures accuracy of information through memorization.
   D. It appears natural and conversational while being well-prepared.

9. What is the primary disadvantage of using a manuscript style of speech delivery?
   A. It lacks accuracy and precision in conveying information.
   B. It often results in excessive use of body language.
   C. It can make the speech sound robotic and less engaging.
   D. It requires extensive memorization of the speech.

10. Why is it important for a speaker to use natural and purposeful body language during a speech?
    A. Because it entertains the audience with flashy gestures.
    B. Because it emphasizes the memorized content of the speech.
    C. Because it conveys a sense of confidence and professionalism.
    D. Because it distracts the audience from the speech content.

11. Good posture is important for a speaker during a presentation because _____.
    A. it allows the speaker to move around the stage more freely
    B. it indicates that the speaker is focused on reading from notes
    C. it signals to the audience that the speaker is confident and serious
    D. it enables the speaker to use flashy and dramatic gestures

12. What is the purpose of using gestures in a speech?
    A. To distract the audience from the content of the speech.
    B. To emphasize and illustrate specific points in the speech.
    C. To replace verbal communication with physical actions.
    D. To create a sense of chaos and unpredictability.

13. Which type of gestures is commonly used to convey specific meanings and often replaces verbal communication?
    A. Illustrator.   B. Regulator.
    C. Emote.   D. Emblem.

14. What is one benefit of maintaining eye contact with the audience during a speech?

   A. It distracts the audience from the content of the speech.

   B. It conveys the speaker's expertise in reading from notes.

   C. It establishes a connection with the audience.

   D. It allows the speaker to focus more on their speech notes.

15. Reading a speech verbatim from a computer screen is discouraged during a virtual presentation because _____.

   A. it is difficult to see the text on the screen.

   B. it makes the speaker appear too focused on the notes.

   C. it distracts the audience from the speaker's face.

   D. it results in a lack of non-verbal communication.

16. What is the recommended approach for using speech notes during a virtual presentation?

   A. Keep the notes on a separate table away from the computer.

   B. Place the notes in the speaker's pocket for easy access.

   C. Attach the notes to the back of the computer screen.

   D. Read the notes directly from a transcript on the computer.

17. It is important not to transcribe a speech verbatim for a virtual presentation because _____.

   A. it takes too much time to create effective speech notes

   B. the audience can easily see that the speaker is reading

   C. the speaker may forget the content of the speech

   D. it makes the speech appear too informal

18. What is a potential consequence of reading a speech verbatim during the online speech presentation?

   A. The audience becomes too engaged with the content.

   B. The speaker's voice becomes more dynamic and expressive.

   C. The audience perceives the speaker as unprepared and lacking engagement.

   D. The non-verbal cues of the speaker become more pronounced.

19. It is important for an impromptu speaker to create and practice speech notes because _____.

   A. it ensures accurate and precise delivery of information

   B. it prevents the audience from noticing a lack of preparation

   C. it enhances non-verbal communication during the speech

   D. it provides a structure and guide for the spontaneous speech

20. What is the primary focus when processing speech notes for the online speech delivery?
   A. Transcribing the speech verbatim for accuracy.
   B. Creating a visually engaging slideshow presentation.
   C. Ensuring the notes are hidden from the audience's view.
   D. Developing effective speech notes to guide the presentation.

11.3 Speaking Task: Running for the President of the Student Union

Task Suppose you are going to deliver a speech to run for the president of the Student Union. Write a speech to demonstrate that you are qualified for the position with at least 300 words. Your speech should include with an introduction, a body and a conclusion.

The following are tips for your reference.

- Give a simple welcome to all student voters;
- Introduce yourself;
- Try to persuade them with the evidence that you are the best choice, including your educational/personal qualifications, your main achievements, or special talents related to the position;
- Tell the voters the common needs at campus that should be fulfilled right away and the measures you are going to take to achieve your goal if you are chosen as the president of the Student Union;
- Conclusion.

11.4 Self-Reflection: Evaluating a Presentation in Talking to the Audience

Evaluate your speech in talking to the audience. Rate your speech on each point: E—excellent, G—good, A—average, F—fair, P—poor.

Checklist: Presentation in Talking to the Audience

Items	Scores					Comments
	E	G	A	F	P	
Eye contact Eye contact throughout the speech						
Tone of voice (1) volume (2) pitch (3) pace						
Body language (1) gestures (2) facial expressions						
Interaction with the audience (1) responsiveness to questions (2) engaging the audience through humor (3) engaging the audience through personal anecdotes						
Clarity of message (1) use of clear language (2) explaining complex ideas in simple terms						

Unit 12

Speaking on Special Occasions

In this unit you will learn to:

- understand the differences between special occasion speeches and informative or persuasive speeches;
- identify major types of special occasion speeches;
- recognize the principles of each type of speeches for special occasions;
- be familiar with the guidelines for speaking on different special occasions.

12.1 Speech Reading: The Tragedy of the Challenger Crew

Activity 1 Lead-in Listening

Listen to the speech and write down the summary.

Activity 2 Pre-reading Questions

1. What do you know about "Challenger Space Shuttle" disaster? Give a brief introduction.

2. If you were an American citizen in 1986, how would you feel about the space program after the tragedy of "Challenger"?

3. Do you think how an inspiring speech can help traumatic people?

The Tragedy of the Challenger① Crew[1]

1 Ladies and Gentlemen, I'd planned to speak to you tonight to report on the state of the Union②, but the events of earlier today have led me to change those plans. Today is a day for **mourning** and remembering. Nancy and I are pained **to the core** by the tragedy of the **shuttle** Challenger. We know we share this pain with all of the people of our country. This is truly a national loss.

---

1 This text is the transcript of a video clip from the Bilibili website.

Unit 12 Speaking on Special Occasions

2   Nineteen years ago, almost to the day, we lost three astronauts in a terrible accident on the ground. But, we've never lost an astronaut in flight. We've never had a tragedy like this. And perhaps we've forgotten the courage it took for the crew of the shuttle. But they, the Challenger Seven, were aware of the dangers, but overcame them and did their jobs brilliantly. We mourn seven heroes: Michael Smith, Dick Scobee, Judith Resnik, Ronald McNair, Ellison Onizuka, Gregory Jarvis, and Christa McAuliffe. We mourn their loss as a nation together.

3   For the families of the seven, we cannot bear, as you do, the full impact of this tragedy. But we feel the loss, and we're thinking about you so very much. Your loved ones were daring and brave, and they had that special grace, that special spirit that says, "Give me a challenge, and I'll meet it with joy." They had a hunger to explore the universe and discover its truths. They wished to serve, and they did. They served all of us.

4   We've grown used to wonders in this century. It's hard to **dazzle** us. But for twenty-five years the United States space program has been doing just that. We've grown used to the idea of space, and, perhaps we forget that we've only just begun. We're still pioneers. They, the members of the Challenger crew, were pioneers.

5   And I want to say something to the schoolchildren of America who were watching the **live coverage** of the shuttle's take-off. I know it's hard to understand, but sometimes painful things like this happen. It's all part of the process of exploration and discovery. It's all part of taking a chance and expanding man's horizons. The future doesn't belong to the **fainthearted**; it belongs to the brave. The Challenger crew was pulling us into the future, and we'll continue to follow them.

6   I've always had great faith in and respect for our space program. And what happened today does nothing to diminish it. We don't hide our space program. We don't keep secrets and cover things up. We do it all up front and in public. That's the way freedom is, and we wouldn't change it for a minute.

7   We'll continue our **quest** in space. There will be more shuttle flights and more shuttle crews and, yes, more volunteers, more civilians, more teachers in space. Nothing ends here; our hopes and our journeys continue.

8   I want to add that I wish I could talk to every man and woman who works for NASA, or who worked on this mission and tell them: "Your dedication and **professionalism** have moved and impressed us for decades. And we know of your anguish. We share it."

9   There's a coincidence today. On this day 390 years ago, the great explorer Sir Francis Drake[③] died aboard ship off the coast of Panama. In his lifetime the great frontiers were the oceans, and a historian later said, "He lived by the sea, died on

199

it, and was buried in it." Well, today, we can say of the Challenger Crew: Their dedication was, like Drake's, complete.

10   The crew of the space shuttle Challenger honored us by the manner in which they lived their lives. We will never forget them, nor the last time we saw them, this morning, as they prepared for their journey and waved goodbye and "slipped the surly bonds of earth" to "touch the face of God".

11   Thank you.

> **Analysis**
>
> The text is a transcript of the speech delivered by former American president Ronald Reagan in January 28th, 1986, in his oval office at White House, mourning the Challenger Crew who just died in the space shuttle tragedy. At the beginning, the President made it very clear that this was a national loss and people all had to mourn and remember the seven heroes. And he emphasized how courageous and dedicated these astronauts were since this was the first record of deaths in flight in the history of American space program. He then extended his compassion and support to the traumatic families. And he highly praised the heroic sacrifice these astronauts made. After that, he particularly addressed to schoolchildren in order to help them to make sense of a painful accident like this one. In the end, he tried to inspire American people at this anguish moment. He called on the whole nation to continue the quest just like what the Challenger Seven wished and what the pioneering spirit guided.
>
> Besides expressing mourning and remembering in the speech, powerful inspiration is a typical feature of commemorative speech like this one. You don't just sink the people in anguish. Instead, you should encourage them to unite in time of sorrow and go on with the journey more courageously. In order to achieve this purpose, the following methods have been used.
>
> ● **Analyzing the occasion**
>
> This speech has been delivered to the nation on the night of the accident. Over the world there were more than 1 billion people watching the space shuttle exploded in the air either at the spot or on TV. So the President mentioned more than once the mourning, the loss, and their courage and dedication. In this way, people, especially their loving families and friends, may feel comforted and supported.
>
> ● **Using rhetorical devices**
>
> Parallelism: "The future doesn't belong to the fainthearted; it belongs to the brave."
>
> Quotation: "He lived by the sea, died on it, and was buried in it."

Unit 12　Speaking on Special Occasions

● **Relating to the audience**

In his speech, President Reagan particularly addressed the schoolchildren. This is because among seven astronauts there was a teacher who planned to have a space class so there were more students around the nation to watch the live broadcasting than usual. The President probably worried about how well the schoolchildren may cope with this tragedy happening in front of their eyes. So he analyzed this and tried to help in his speech.

Useful Words & Expressions

dazzle	v.	使人目眩；留下深刻印象
fainthearted	adj.	懦弱的，胆小的
mourn	v.	悼念，哀悼
professionalism	n.	敬业，专业精神
quest	n.	寻求，探求；探险
shuttle	n.	航天飞机
live coverage		现场报道
to the core		彻头彻尾地，完全地

Notes

① the Challenger: It refers to the Challenger space shuttle, which was launched on January 28, 1986, at Eastern Standard Time in the United States. It disintegrated 73 seconds after liftoff, and all seven astronauts on board perished. They are known as the "Challenger Crew" or "Challenger Seven".

② the state of the Union Address: According to American custom, at the beginning of each year, the incumbent president delivers an annual report to Congress, outlining the government's policy direction, known as the State of the Union address. This address primarily clarifies the domestic and international situations the president faces each year, as well as the policies and measures the government intends to implement.

③ Sir Francis Drake: He was an English privateer and explorer, as well as a politician during the Elizabethan era. Drake undertook two circumnavigations in 1577 and 1580 and was awarded the title of Knight by Queen Elizabeth I, who personally boarded his ship for the honor.

Critical Thinking

1. How do the purposes of special occasion speeches differ from those of informative or persuasive speeches?

2. How do a speech align with the goal of its occasion?

3. How do cultural factors influence the content and delivery of special occasion speeches? What steps can a speaker take to ensure his or her speech is culturally appropriate and respectful?

4. In special occasion speeches, how can a speaker balance any informative or persuasive elements with the primary goal of creating an evocative atmosphere? What strategies can be used to integrate these elements seamlessly?

5. How can a speaker forge a meaningful connection with the audience when delivering a speech like "The Tragedy of the Challenger Crew" on a special occasion?

12.2 Skill Focus: Types of and Principles for Special Occasion Speeches

Besides the informative speech and persuasive speech, there are other types of speeches. Certain types of speeches have nothing to do with informing or persuading an audience; instead, special occasions require various types of speeches. Whether you are giving a toast or a eulogy; whether you want to pay tribute or to present awards, knowing how to create an effective and evocative aura in different contexts is fundamental in special occasion speeches.

12.2.1 Speech of Introduction

The speech of introduction, by definition, is delivered to introduce someone on a special occasion or for an event. Compared with other types of speeches, it can be relatively short. Although you introduce someone in just one sentence, the audience will be least interested in the speech. So your speech of introduction should arouse the audience's curiosity and make the main speaker feel welcomed.

An effective speech of introduction should at least include three key points. (1) Build up the main speaker's credibility. You want the audience to feel like listening to the speaker. (2) To introduce the topic to the audience and to leave an impression on the audience before the speech will help them to remember after it. (3) Create an welcoming climate for the main speaker. A warm and friendly atmosphere can help to ease the speaker's anxiety as well as build up the confidence.

No matter how succinct your speech of introduction is, it should still be a complete speech with a full introduction-body-conclusion structure as shown in the following table.

Sample Structure of a Speech of Introduction

	Contents	Detailed Information: Examples
Introduction	Hook/attention getter (things that make the audience interested and excited about the main speaker)	Information about the main speaker the introducer has read; The speaker's main lecture(s) the introducer has been impressed or attended; Achievements or awards; ...
(Transition)		
Body	Topic; Credibility	Speech title and some information about the topic; Qualification of the main speaker;
(Transition)		
Conclusion	Welcome	Hand off the stage to the main speaker and welcome he or she by clapping and shaking hands.

Here are some tips for the speech of introduction. You should gather enough information before the event. Ask the speaker for biographical information you can share in the introduction. Notice that the information should be closely related to the topic, but there's no need listing every bit of the speaker's personal life and achievement. You may check online or ask people who know the speaker for the information you want to cover. Ask the speaker for the title of the speech. Get to know something about the topic before the speech.

12.2.2 Speech of Presentation

A speech of presentation is a brief speech for presenting a prize, award, or honor. Speeches of presentation can be simple including only one sentence or can last up to 5–6 minutes. So the first thing the speaker needs to find out is the time limit of the presentation speech. If you are aware of how long your speech should be, then you can set out crafting your speech as the following steps: (1) greet the audience; (2) explain what the prize/award/honor is and why it's important; (3) explain why the recipient deserves it; (4) present the prize/award/honor; (5) wish the recipient well. These five steps may not be practiced in all cases. If it's an well-known event such as Nobel Prize, then no explanation as for "What is it?" is needed. In addition, if it is a race or competition conducted on a public platform and numerous people don't win, you may want to recognize and thank the work of other competitors or nominees for their efforts as well.

12.2.3 Speech of Acceptance

An acceptance speech, given by the recipient of a prize or honor, is complementary to a speech of presentation. Although the recipients can say whatever they want, there are still some typical points should be included.

First, thank the people who have given you the award or honor. Thank those who have voted for you as well if possible.

Second, thank the people who have made contribution to your achievement. It's a good opportunity to recognize their efforts and supports in public.

Third, give a unique perspective to your speech. Tell the audience why this prize or honor is meaningful to you. Focusing on one point can make it a good acceptance speech. Keep in mind the principles for acceptance speeches: be grateful and graceful and be short.

12.2.4 Toast

Toast is also one type of public speaking, so it should follow the typical pattern. The introduction part and conclusion part of the toast should highlight the same theme. Meanwhile, add influence to your language using rhetorical devices such as parallel structure.

Toast is designed for the purpose of congratulating, appreciating and remembering at festive occasions. It can be delivered at some personal occasions such as weddings, retirement parties or farewell parties, and they can also be more publicly delivered on diplomatic or business occasions. Here are some tips toast speakers should pay attention to.

(1) Make your toast special. A toast is delivered to honor a person or a favorable occasion, so the main purpose is to make the person or the occasion become special.

(2) Make your toast short. Your toast is made for the celebration, so don't take the festivity away with many remarks.

(3) Make your toast specific. When you are invited to make a toast on a special

occasion, it usually means you are personally close and important either to the person or to the event. So your toast speech must be personal and specific. Do not ramble about things too broadly.

(4) As for some diplomatic or international business occasions, toast speeches should be longer, and the remarks should be delivered with sincerity, clarity and succinctness. Besides celebrating the festive atmosphere, a toast made to international guests should also clarify your side's principles and standpoints.

(5) If it's an international occasion, pay attention to the pronunciation of the foreign expressions and cultural taboos beforehand.

These tips should be of some help, but if you want to take your speech to the next level, you should polish your language. The toast should sound more advanced with a theme. There's no need for your toast to cover every single detail of the person or the occasion. Rather, the details and pieces of information should be organized under one integrated theme. This will definitely leave a deep impression on the audience's minds.

12.2.5 Commemorative Speech

The purpose of a commemorative speech is to commemorate an extraordinary person, a group of people, and an important thing or idea. Commemorative speeches allow you to pay tribute publicly by honoring, remembering, or memorializing. A commemorative speech stands out of other types of special occasion speeches because it should contain some elements of informative speeches. This is designed to inform the audience why the topic is worth valuing and commemorating. Therefore, the common skills will also fit here, such as the use of statistics or examples. But what's different is that a commemorative speech aims at inspiring the audience rather than informing them. The speech will be a successful one only when the audience feel like respecting and admiring the person, the institution or the idea. In order to do so, you should express their emotions and have the audience resonate with you.

Here are some tips to make a commemorative speech. (1) Make the audience feel involved. The more they feel involved, the more likely they will resonate with the speaker. (2) Make details magnified. Focus on the details in life and make them feel larger for the audience. If the audience is attracted and concentrated on the details, they tend to attach importance to them and ignore the fact that they are trivial. (3) Make pictures in the audience's minds by telling stories with vividness. Details and vivid description can help the audience to establish concrete understanding of ideas, events, and characters.

> **Exercises**

Choose the best options to answer the following questions or fill in the blanks based on the information according to the Skill Focus in this unit.

1. The speech of introduction is an address that introduces the main speaker. So the introducer is supposed to _____.
   A. introduce the speaker in one short sentence like "Today's speaker is..."
   B. praise the speaker and pay tribute to him or her
   C. establish a welcoming climate that will boost the speaker's credibility
   D. introduce the speaker in the same way even to two different groups

2. In order not to embarrass himself or herself as well as the main speaker in the speech of introduction, the introducer should always do the following EXCEPT _____.
   A. getting the speaker's name right
   B. making sure the remarks are accurate
   C. hesitating to think about the facts if he or she not sure when introducing
   D. delivering the introduction without any error

3. Which of the following occasions requires a formal introduction?
   A. A formal banquet.
   B. A private business meeting.
   C. A meeting between two distinguished scholars.
   D. An in-classroom lecture by a guest professor.

4. All of the following are the objectives of speech introduction EXCEPT _____.
   A. getting the attention and interest of your audience
   B. reinforcing the central idea
   C. previewing the body of the speech
   D. creating a positive relationship with the audience

5. When the introducer mentions personal information of the speaker, it will result in _____.
   A. helping to relate to the audience
   B. building up the enthusiasm for the speaker
   C. creating a set of expectations for the speaker
   D. making the speaker uncomfortable because the personal information may be painful rather than funny to the speaker

6. Which of the following is TRUE of the introduction of a speech?
   A. The speaker can easily get the audience's attention by looking directly at the

audience without saying a word for a while.
   B. Under normal circumstances, the introductory part constitutes more than 20% of your speech.
   C. The speaker should always apologize when he or she feels nervous.
   D. The speaker should start the speech as soon as possible.

7. A speaker introducing an author of academic writing to the audience of enthusiastic readers will best accomplish this goal by _____.
   A. praising the author as the finest public speaker in academic world
   B. summarizing the author's major works and accomplishments in writing
   C. presenting a detailed biography of the author's entire life
   D. discussing the author's educational background and work experiences

8. What should you do to adapt to the audience?
   A. As long as you prepare hard ahead of time, things will go exactly as planned on the day of your speech.
   B. During the speech, you should deliver it the same way even if you have less time available.
   C. Be sure to keep an eye out for the audience feedback during the speech.
   D. It seems quite strange to think of the audience adaptation after the speech.

9. You should begin the speech in all following ways EXCEPT _____.
   A. always using a well-known or famous quotation
   B. starting with short quotations since lengthy ones will set the audience yawning
   C. beginning with a provocative, dramatic or suspenseful story that are relevant to the topic
   D. asking the audience a rhetoric question to get them to think about the speech

10. Which one of the following statements is TRUE?
    A. A speech of introduction should be as brief as less than a sentence.
    B. The objective of a speech of presentation is to acknowledge the recipient's achievements.
    C. A good acceptance speech counts on how well the speaker introduces his or her achievements to get the award.
    D. Speeches for special occasions are nothing different from other types of public speaking.

11. Which of the following is an example of a speech for a special occasion?
    A. A speech presenting an award to a retiring police officer.
    B. A presentation on marketing strategy at a sales meeting.
    C. A talk to college freshmen about how to register for classes.
    D. A lecture by a visiting professor in a college class

12. Which one is NOT what the speaker should do in a toast?
    A. Saying a few words of greeting, celebration or thanks in conjunction with a meal or reception.
    B. Always ending your toast with the same phrase "Cheers".
    C. Delivering a reciprocal toast with sincerity and warmth in a formal diplomatic or international business banquet.
    D. Rising from your chair and speaking to the entire room when delivering the toast.

13. Which of the following is typically included in an acceptance speech after winning an award?
    A. A detailed explanation of the award criteria.
    B. A thank to other nominees for the competition and admiration for their work.
    C. A comprehensive list of all the nominee's career achievements.
    D. A critique of the judging process.

14. According to the text, a speech in which an individual gives thanks for a gift or award is termed a(n) _____.
    A. speech of presentation
    B. commemorative speech
    C. after-dinner speech
    D. acceptance speech

15. Which of the following statements is NOT true?
    A. A toast should rarely exceed three to five minutes.
    B. You should rise from your chair and speak to the entire room.
    C. The toast is the oldest speech in the world.
    D. You should make eye contact with the honored person while giving the toast.

16. As it's put in the textbook, no speech depends more on the creative and subtle use of language than does the _____.
    A. commemorative speech
    B. speech of presentation
    C. speech of introduction
    D. persuasive speech

17. If you attended an award ceremony and heard the following speeches, which one would be an example of a commemorative speech?
    A. A speech explaining the history of the Oscar Statue.
    B. A speech presenting all the candidates for Best Students of the Year on campus.

C. A speech accepting the Medal of the Republic.

D. A speech honoring Yuan Longping for his lifetime contribution.

18. Today we still find commemorative speeches like the Gettysburg Address meaningful and inspiring primarily_____.
    A. because of the eloquent use of language
    B. because of the occasions on which they were delivered
    C. because they were delivered by very important celebrities
    D. because they were delivered from the memory

19. The following statements are all true for a toast EXCEPT that _____.
    A. a toast can be very brief or longer and more complex on different occasions
    B. the custom of saying a few words of greeting, celebration or thanks is quite common
    C. it's acceptable if you have wrong pronunciation or use inappropriate phrases when making a toast in a cross-cultural situation
    D. the toast is one of the oldest speeches in the world

20. Which of the following statements about speeches on special occasions is TRUE?
    A. Nelson Mandela delivered a short, humble but gracious speech accepting the Congressional Gold Medal which exemplifies the major traits of a good acceptance speech.
    B. A commemorative speech can only be delivered in honor of celebrities, not ordinary persons.
    C. In a speech of introduction, the introducer should be clearly introduced before the main speaker.
    D. When presenting the winner of a world photo contest, the host gave a detailed account of every piece of the winner's past accomplishments.

12.3 Speaking Task: Making a Speech on a Special Occasion

Task Design a special prize for one of your classmates. And you are supposed to deliver a speech of presentation of the prize. Write down a draft within 120 words and deliver it to the class.

12.4 Self-Reflection: Evaluating Your Special Occasion Speech

Evaluate your speech based on how well you meet each specific criterion during your speech. Rate your speech on each point: E—excellent, G—good, A—average, F—fair, P—poor.

Checklist: Special Occasion Speech

Items	\multicolumn{5}{c}{Scores}	Comments
	E	G	A	F	P	
Topic Adapt to the occasion Adapt to the audience Achieve creativity in the speech						
Organization Introduction: to gain attention and interest Main ideas: easy to follow Conclusion: memorable Transition and connectives have been used						
Language Clear and concrete Vivid and colorful Appropriate to the topic, audience and occasion						
Delivery No rushing in beginning and ending Effective pause, rate, pitch, and vocal variety Avoid detaching physical action Maintain strong eye contact						

(To be continued)

(Continued)

Items	Scores					Comments
	E	G	A	F	P	
Overall Assessment						
Which part is the most satisfactory one of the speech?						
Which part is the least satisfactory one of the speech?						
If you were to deliver the speech again, how would you improve it?						

教师服务

感谢您选用清华大学出版社的教材！为了更好地服务教学，我们为授课教师提供本学科重点教材信息及样书，请您扫码获取。

≫ 最新书目

扫码获取 2024 **外语类** 重点教材信息

≫ 样书赠送

教师扫码即可获取样书